Foreword

The Bail Process Project arose from concern about defendants who commit offences while they are on bail before trial. It formed part of a package of measures that were announced by the government in 1992. An earlier report by Burrows, Henderson and Morgan described the first phase of the project in which a detailed descriptive study was carried out of the process by which information on defendants is obtained and the question of bail is decided. Local inter-agency working groups in the five participating court areas identified any problems that there were in the process and set in hand the changes that were possible to remedy these.

This report describes the later phase of the project in which a quantitative study of offending on bail was carried out in the five areas. Comparisons were made of the rates of offending on bail before and after the changes were made, while account was taken of the relevant characteristics of the defendants involved. The results were mixed. Two areas showed a reduction in the rates of offending on bail while the other three showed little change. Analysis showed that the factors which were most associated with offending on bail were the waiting time before trial, homelessness, the current offence charged, the previous criminal history and the previous record on bail of the defendant. An exercise held in one court as part of a magistrates' training programme made it possible to describe the views of magistrates and other remand decision-makers of which types on defendants were more likely to offend on bail.

DAVID MOXON
Head of the Crime and Criminal Justice Unit

Acknowledgements

We would like to thank all those who have assisted in the research described in this report. We are particularly grateful to the five Justices Clerks of the magistrates' courts that took part (Bournemouth, Horseferry Road, Leicester City, Newport and Salford) for chairing the local working groups and making the research possible; to all those members of the criminal justice agencies in the study areas who took on the extra burden of recording data on individual cases for the project (namely, the magistrates, court clerks, CPS prosecutors, police officers, bail information officers and defence solicitors); to Jenny Warren and Jason Preece, whose diligent labours with criminal records produced the information on offending on bail; and to Mamta Ranji, Nicola Dowds and Tim Edwards who gave invaluable assistance with preparation of the data.

We are indebted to Patricia Hassett who led the exercise on decision-making described in Chapter 3, and to John Burrows who, as the consultant to the earlier part of the project, laid the groundwork for the currrent research.

Finally, we are grateful to Anthea Hucklesby, Emma Marshall and Jenny Warren for the follow-up research on the effects of the Criminal Justice and Public Order Act 1994, summarised in Appendix E.

PATRICIA MORGAN
PAUL HENDERSON

Contents

Summary

The aim of the Bail Process Project was to improve the quality, accuracy and timeliness of the information available to remand decision-makers so that they were better able to assess the risk of offending on bail.

Inter-agency working groups were set up in five court areas in 1992. Each group, chaired by the Justices' Clerk, studied the remand process in its own area, and identified problems that affected the information available to the police custody officers, CPS prosecutors and magistrates when they made a pre-trial decision or recommendation on bail or custody. The groups then set in hand the changes that were possible to solve these problems.

The problems that were identified are described by Burrows et al. (1994) and are summarised in Appendix A of this report. The main changes that were introduced by the courts were as follows.

- In most areas, the early *availability of the defendant's criminal record* was a problem. One area was able to extend the hours of direct access to its local records from eight to twenty-four hours a day. Another negotiated access to the more detailed record held by the National Identification Service (as compared with the brief record held on the police national computer). A third area was able to establish a mechanism whereby the court was informed if the defendant was already on bail from a different police station or court within the same police force area.

- All five areas carried out some *training of magistrates in risk assessment,* and ways of improving magistrates' awareness of bail hostel facilities in the area were explored. Three areas set up *training courses for police custody officers* on the same topic to ensure greater uniformity of practice.

- Three areas amended the *wording of bail conditions of residence or curfew,* to oblige the defendant to present himself or herself in person to police officers monitoring his/her compliance. Three areas distributed *simplified bail notices* to make the terms of bail clearer to defendants, that is, the date of the next court appearance and any conditions attached. These were issued to defendants granted unconditional bail as well as those granted bail with conditions.

- In two areas, court clerks started to keep *a record of representations made in remand decisions* so that future benches would know the reasons why earlier decisions had been made.

- Two areas made changes in court listing times to allow more *time for pre-court discussion between the agencies* and, in one area, new arrangements allowed Saturday courts to have access to the probation service.

- In two areas, local steering mechanisms were established under the Court User Group to ensure *better liaison between two bail information schemes in the same area,* and to ensure general understanding of how negative information (that which might work against the granting of bail) was handled by the probation service (see Appendix D).

- In single areas, the following changes were made: a *new prison-based bail information scheme* and a *trial bail support scheme* for 18- to 25-year-olds were established; a scheme was set up to provide *volunteers to act as 'appropriate adults'* during police interviews with under-17-year-olds; and arrangements were made for a *review panel for mentally disordered offenders.*

Case tracking data were collected on cases involving bail/custody decisions in the five areas over a period of three months in 1993 and three months in 1994 (before and after the improvements suggested above). Defendants released on bail in the two samples of cases were followed up at the criminal records office to find details of any offences that were committed while they were on bail.

Analyses showed that the *proportion of defendants granted court bail who were convicted of an offence committed while they were on bail* was reduced in two of the court areas, and changed only slightly or not at all in the other three. The clear decreases were in the Horseferry Road court area (from 18% in 1993 to 11% in 1994), and in the Leicester court area (from 20% in 1993 to 12% in 1994). The proportion of persons *charged with offences committed on court bail* showed similar decreases: in Horseferry Road area from 22 per cent to 16 per cent, and in Leicester, from 24 per cent to 16 per cent.

The analyses suggest that offending on bail decreased in the Horseferry Road area because more persons were remanded in custody (the custody rates increased by six percentage points between 1993 and 1994). Leicester showed a different picture in that the custody rates went down by about five percentage points. This suggests that the reduction in offending on bail in Leicester may have been caused by some of the improvements made, such as better access to defendant's bail history, or an increased emphasis on the training of magistrates in the assessment of risk.

The analyses also showed that the rates of offending while on police bail after charge (as measured by convictions) showed a small decrease overall from nine per cent to eight per cent. There were small decreases in three areas, between two and three percentage points, no change in Newport and a small increase in Bournemouth. Bournemouth and Salford showed the lowest rates for offending on police bail (between 5% and 8%): for Salford this is probably explained by the fact that this area was found to have a much higher rate of police custody after charge (see Chapter 4).

The rates of offending on police bail as measured by charges showed a similar pattern with slightly higher figures. Over all areas, the rates changed from 12 per cent in 1993 to 11 per cent in 1994.

An exercise was carried out with bail decision-makers in Leicester to explore their approach to assessing risk. This established a set of factors which were held to be important, and explored how these were seen to be related to the assessment of the risk of the defendant failing to appear at court and the risk of offending while on bail (see Tables 3.1 and 3.2).

The case tracking data were analysed to explore which categories of defendant were associated with higher and lower than average rates of offending on court bail. Those with higher rates included defendants:

• with no fixed abode (42% offended on bail)

• charged with car theft or burglary (32%, 29% respectively offended on bail)

• who waited more than six months before trial (32%) or more than three months (24%)

• aged 17 and under (29%)

• who had served a previous custodial sentence (28%)

• who had a previous record of breaching bail (27%)

• who were unemployed (21%).

Those with lower rates were those:

- who waited less than a month before trial (4%)

- who were in employment (7%)

- who were charged with assault (7%) or fraud (8%)

- who were 21 or over (13%).

(Rates for combinations of these factors are shown in Table 5.3.)

1 Introduction

The Bail Process Project arose from concern about the extent of offending on bail. In 1992, there was a great deal of public discussion of the issue when three police forces published a range of figures from surveys carried out in their own areas, and the Home Office published results from its internal research.[1] The then Home Secretary gave an undertaking to Parliament to tackle this issue by setting up pilot projects in selected local areas. The intention was to improve the quality of the information available to the courts to assist them in identifying those defendants who were most likely to offend on bail.

This commitment led to a steering committee being set up which included representatives from all the relevant criminal justice agencies, i.e. the police, the Crown Prosecution Service (CPS), the magistrates' courts, the probation service and the Law Society. The committee was to tackle two main tasks:

* to investigate what information was required by remand decision-makers, and in what ways the information available was judged to be deficient

* to explore ways of remedying these deficiencies and, where possible, to put these remedies into effect.

Background: who makes pre-trial decisions

In England and Wales, the majority of decisions about the granting of bail before trial arise at three points: when a suspect has been arrested by the police but the evidence available is not sufficient for charges to be brought; when a suspect has been arrested and charged with an offence; and when the court has decided to adjourn the hearing of a case to another date. The first two of these decisions are made by the police: the third is made by magistrates.

---

1 The Metropolitan Police (Ennis and Nichols, 1991). Avon and Somerset Constabulary (Brookes, 1991) and Northumbria (Northumbria Police, 1991). New Home Office research on the topic was reported by Henderson (Henderson and Nicols, 1992) and Morgan (1992). Earlier work on the topic had been done by Greater Manchester Police, 1988)

When a suspect has been arrested but the police do not have sufficient evidence to charge him (or her)[2] with an offence, they can either release him without charge or, if they wish to seek more evidence before deciding whether to charge, they can release him with the requirement that he returns to the police station on a given date. This second alternative is usually called bail to return to the police station.[3] It differs from the other types of bail considered in this report in that, once the initial questioning is concluded, the police have no option of holding the suspect in custody.

After a suspect has been charged with an offence, the police must decide whether he (the 'defendant') should be held in custody overnight to appear at the next available magistrates' court, or whether he can be released on bail with the requirement that he appears at the court on a given date.[4] (This type of bail will be called police bail after charge.) The information on which this decision is based will be obtained from the defendant himself, from the arresting police officer, possibly from statements by witnesses to the offence, and from the criminal records office on the defendant's past record. At this stage, the police may also make a recommendation to the CPS as to whether the defendant should be refused bail at his first appearance in court.

A defendant who is held in police custody overnight may be interviewed next day by a 'bail information officer' (BIO) who will check on any information he supplies, such as details of home address and employment.[5] If the defendant is homeless, the BIO will try to arrange accommodation for him. The BIO will then pass the verified information to the CPS before the court hearing. Where there is no such bail information scheme, the court probation officer will try to arrange accommodation for homeless defendants.

When the defendant appears at court, the case might be dealt with immediately, in which case no further pre-trial decisions are needed. In many cases, however, this is not possible and the court will adjourn the proceedings to a future date. When they adjourn a case, the magistrates

---

2   In the remainder of this report, the male gender will be used as a shorthand to refer to males or females.

3   This type of bail, defined in section 47(3) of the Police and Criminal Act, 1985, is granted under section 34 (5) of the same Act. As a shorthand, it is sometimes referred to by practioners as section 47 (3) bail and sometimes as section 34 (5) bail. Both shorthand descriptions refer to the same type of bail.

4   Since April 1995, the police have had the power to grant bail with conditions as an alternative to granting unconditional bail (from section 27 of the CJPO Act, 1994). However, the exercises and data collection described in chapters 2 to 5 were carried out before this date, when the police only had two options, to hold in custody or grant unconditional bail. Raine and Wilson (1996) looked at the effects of the new powers in six police stations. See also the survey of custody officers in Appendix E of this report.

5   Bail information officers work as part of bail information schemes, which are run by the probation service. Such schemes are not available in all parts of the country. Where there are schemes, they are either based on the court, as described above, or they are based on the local prison or remand centre. In prison-based schemes, the bail information officer will interview defendants when they have already been remanded in custody by the courts, and the information collected will be given to the courts at the second remand hearing rather than the first. More details of bail information schemes are given by Godson and Mitchell (1991), Lloyd (1992) and Lloyd and Mair (1996).

must decide whether to remand the defendant on bail or in custody until the next hearing. They will first hear any recommendations by the CPS prosecutor, usually in the form of any 'objections to bail' which the CPS wish to make. The defence lawyer will then be given the opportunity to make representations to the magistrates before their decision is made.

Magistrates can choose between three alternatives:

- they can grant the defendant unconditional bail, the only requirement being that he must appear at court again on the date specified

- they can grant bail with specific conditions attached, such as a requirement to live at a given address, to observe a curfew or to report daily to the police station

- or they can order that the defendant be held in custody until the next court hearing.

Grounds for and consequences of pre-trial decisions

The grounds on which the police can refuse bail after charge to a defendant are set out in section 38 of the Police and Criminal Evidence Act, 1985 (PACE). The grounds on which the court can refuse bail are set out in schedule one of the Bail Act, 1976. The most important grounds are that, if released on bail, the defendant would be likely to:

- fail to appear at the next court appearance

- commit an offence while on bail[6]

- interfere with the witnesses who will be giving evidence against him or otherwise obstruct the course of justice.

In making their decision or recommendation, the police, CPS and court are required to assess the risk that any of the above will occur. If they lean too far on the side of leniency, the result may be that more people will fail to appear at court (hence avoiding justice), more offences will be committed by persons on bail (causing nuisance or positive danger to the public), and/or more witnesses will be intimidated.

---

6   At the time this project was carried out, the wording in PACE was that the defendant would cause 'loss or damage to property'. The CJPO Act, 1994 gave the police the additional power to detain if they considered that the defendant was likely to commit offences if granted bail. Appendix E of this report gives more information on the new power.

On the other hand, if the decision-makers lean too far on the side of severity, more people are likely to be remanded in custody who would not have 'failed bail' if they had been given the chance. The result will then be that more people will lose their liberty and the prison population will be increased (at some considerable cost) with no consequent benefit to the public.

It is important therefore that decision-makers should try to target those who would fail to appear at court, offend on bail or interfere with witnesses, and remand those persons and those only in custody.

Methodology used in the Bail Process Project

The project involved four approaches.

- Local steering groups were set up which included members of the main criminal justice agencies in five study areas. These groups worked with a consultant appointed by the Home Office. Their task was to describe how the system of pre-trial decision-making worked in their areas, to identify any problems that there were with the information available at each stage of the process, and to suggest improvements that might be made.

- Sessions were held with bail decision-makers in one of the five areas to explore their approach to assessing risk: in particular, to see which factors were held to be important and how these were related to the assessment of risk.

- Data were collected on cases involving bail/custody decisions in the five areas over a period of three months in 1993 and three months in 1994 (i.e., before and after the improvements suggested above were made).[7] Statistical analyses were carried out to assess what specific types of information affected the decisions made, and their relative importance.

- The defendants released on bail in the two samples of cases were followed up at the criminal records office to find details of any offences that were committed during the periods of bail.

---

7   This was known as the case tracking exercise.

Structure of the report

Chapter 2 gives an overview of the Bail Process Project, including the first phase in which the system was described, the improvements put in place in the areas, and the effects of these.

Chapter 3 describes the exercise conducted in one area to explore the views of magistrates (and other agencies involved in the remand decision) on the information they need and how it is used.

Chapter 4 describes the analyses of the case tracking data. In particular, the factors that were associated with specific remand decisions are examined.

Chapter 5 gives more details of the levels of offending on bail found in the five areas. In this section, the data from 1993 and 1994 are amalgamated and the factors associated with higher and lower rates of offending while on bail are given.

In Chapter 6, the conclusions drawn from the studies described in the report are discussed.

2 Design and effects

The design of the project

Five court areas were chosen to take part in the study. These represented the large metropolitan areas of Central London (Horseferry Road court) and Greater Manchester (Salford court), and also the East Midlands (Leicester City court), South Wales (Newport court) and the South Coast (Bournemouth and Poole courts taken together). In each area, the Justices' Clerk was asked to chair a steering group on which the local criminal justice agencies were represented, i.e., the police, CPS, probation service, defence solicitors and, in some areas, the prison service. An independent consultant, John Burrows, was appointed to work with the local groups and address three main objectives:

- to draw up a 'narrative map' which would describe broadly how the system worked in each area with regard to bail/custody decisions

- to identify any problems that there were in the supply of relevant information to bail decision-makers in the area

- to propose changes that might be made to help solve the problems identified and to implement these changes.

Agencies in the five areas were also asked to take part in a case tracking exercise so that there could be a quantitative evaluation of the effects of the project. The police and CPS supplied details of each defendant charged during a three-month period in 1993 – before any changes were made – and repeated the process in a three-month period in 1994, after the changes were in place.

The data collected included personal details of the defendants and their offences, together with details of the bail/custody decisions that were made by the police or magistrates, and recommendations made by the CPS. The researchers later followed up these defendants in the National Identification Service (NIS) at Scotland Yard, with the aim of recording any offences that were committed while the defendants were on police or court bail.

The narrative map

The narrative map was described in detail by Burrows (Burrows et al., 1994). A summary of the main findings is given in Appendix A of this report.

Problems identified by the local steering groups

The local groups identified a range of areas in which improvements were needed.

Access to criminal records. All areas saw a need for improved access. Whereas national criminal records were held by the NIS section of the Metropolitan Police, local records (i.e. records of crimes committed in one police area) were held by the four forces outside London. Access to these local records was usually faster than access to the national system. However, a new national service was then being developed, the Phoenix system, which subsequently started operation in 1995. In the new system, much of the information which had formerly been held on microfiches was to be computerised, but conversion of these back records would take time. Once the new system was developed, some of the existing problems were expected to be solved, but this was outside the timescale for the Bail Process Project. The Phoenix system should also give information on the bail history of defendants.

Pre-court discussions. The shortage of time all parties experienced before the start of a court session was raised. The first issue here was the time at which the prosecutor received the files for overnight custody cases from the police. Adequate preparation time was needed. The second was the time at which various agencies arrived at court, so that consultation was possible between the Crown Prosecutor, the bail information officer and the defence lawyer, before the start of a court session.

Defendants' understanding of the terms of bail. A need was seen for the defendant to be given a simple document which gave the date of his next court appearance and a clear statement of any conditions which were attached to his bail (a 'bail notice'). He would then have no excuse for failing to appear at court or for failing to comply with the bail conditions imposed. The existing forms which gave this information tended to use legal phraseology which many defendants did not find easy to understand. Also, in some areas, these forms had previously only been given to defendants who had been granted conditional bail.

Bail conditions. Several problems were identified. The first concerned the way in which the police were informed about conditions imposed: some police officers reported that they only knew that defendants were required to report to the police station when they actually did so. Another problem was how the compliance with conditions was monitored: police visiting a defendant's home, to check if he was observing a curfew or a condition of residence, were sometimes told that he was at home but was in bed asleep. Three courts modified their standard curfew conditions to include a requirement for the defendant to present himself to any police officer who called to check on him.

The training of police custody officers. A need for greater uniformity of practice was recognised. Only a minority (23%) of the 64 custody officers surveyed in the first phase of the project had had training in bail decision-making. More than 80 per cent felt the need for more training (see Burrows et al., 1994).

Training for magistrates in bail decision-making. Several groups saw a need for more such training. A new training scheme produced by the Magistrates' Association (the Bail Risk Exercise) was then available. This concentrated on ways of assessing the risks set out in the Bail Act (see Chapter 1).

Bail hostels. A need was seen for magistrates to be given more information about the local bail hostels and the national standards that exist for such hostels. Visits to bail hostels were to be encouraged.

Bail information schemes. Issues arose from the running of such schemes, which were in existence in three of the five areas, i.e., in Horseferry Road, Leicester and Bournemouth. The police and CPS needed to be fully aware of the existence and method of working of schemes in their area. There was a need for co-operation when two schemes worked in the same area (i.e. a court based and a prison based scheme). Agreements were needed on how negative information, i.e., that which might act against the granting of bail, was handled. (Appendix D gives more information about the operation of bail information schemes.) One area (Newport) was served by a bail support scheme for defendants aged under 18. Other areas saw advantage in such schemes.[1]

Records of argument in bail decisions. There was seen to be a need for a record to be kept of the representations made in remand hearings (even when they were not contested). Benches at future hearings would then know the reason why specific decisions were made.

---

1   Bail support schemes aim to give support to defendants during their periods of bail, primarily to help them observe any conditions attached to bail, to develop work opportunities, to use leisure time creatively, and to prevent reoffending.

Evaluation : offending on bail and remand decisions

As the project was set up to answer concerns about offending on bail, the Steering Committee asked that the extent of such offending should be measured in the five areas both before and after the local changes had been introduced.

The measures of offending on bail used in this study are:

- the proportion of persons granted bail, and convicted of the original offence,[2] who were *convicted* of an offence committed while they were on bail – this is the main measure of offending on bail that was used in the study (offending on bail conviction rates)

- the proportion of persons granted bail who were *charged* with an offence committed while they were on bail – regardless of whether or not they were convicted either of the original offence or of the offence committed while on bail (offending on bail charge rates).

Neither measure included offences for which the defendant was cautioned, or those which were taken into consideration by the courts (TICs). Such offences are not recorded by the NIS.

The second measure provides a check on the changes in the first measure, as it is not subject to as many methodological difficulties: in particular, it does not depend on the final outcomes of cases being received at the criminal records office (see Appendix C). This measure will, however, tend to overestimate the levels of known offending on bail, as it will include cases in which the charge was withdrawn or the defendant was acquitted of the offence.

Of course neither measure will include offending for which the offender was not caught and so will tend to underestimate the true extent of offending on bail. But, if the offender is not known, nothing can be determined as to whether specific offences were committed by persons on bail.

The study looked at offending by persons who were on bail granted by the courts (court bail) and also by those on bail granted by the police after charge. The original intention was to include offending on bail to return to the police station, but this proved not to be possible because the recording of this type of bail in the exercise was incomplete.

---

2   The measure had to be limited to those convicted of the original offence for methodological reasons described in Appendix C.

Table 2.1 (columns one and two) shows that the offending on *court* bail conviction rate decreased from 20 per cent in the 1993 sample to 15 per cent in the 1994 sample, i.e., five percentage points. The offending on *police* bail conviction rate (columns three and four) showed a small reduction from nine per cent in 1993 to eight per cent in 1994. Analysis described in Chapter 5 suggests that the lower levels of offending on police bail are a result of the shorter periods of time spent on police bail, usually less than six weeks compared with three months or more on court bail.

As regards court bail, it is clear that the overall decrease in the offending on bail conviction rates arose from decreases in two areas, namely, Horseferry Road (from 18% in 1993 to 11% in 1994) and Leicester (from 20% in 1993 to 12% in 1994). The rates in the other three areas changed very little. (Some variation between the percentages measured at different times would be expected because of the relatively small sample sizes.)

Table 2.1 Offending on bail conviction rates in 1993 and 1994 (sample sizes are given in brackets)

Court area	Percent convicted of an offence committed while on COURT bail		Percent convicted of an offence committed while on POLICE bail	
	1993	1994	1993	1994
Bournemouth	16% (178)	16% (226)	6% (243)	8% (446)
Horseferry Rd	18% (191)	11% (207)	11% (236)	9% (99)
Leicester	20% (485)	12% (439)	11% (809)	8% (767)
Newport	18% (132)	17% (131)	9% (467)	9% (480)
Salford	23% (185)	25% (175)	7% (171)	5% (80)
All areas	20% (1,171)	15% (1,178)	9% (1,926)	8% (1,872)

Evidence to support the changes (or lack of changes) in the above table is provided by Table 2.2, which gives the second measure of offending on bail – the offending on bail charge rate. In Horseferry Road, 22 per cent were charged with an offence committed on bail in the 1993 sample compared with 16 per cent in the 1994 sample, a decrease of six percentage points. Similarly there was a decrease in Leicester from 24 per cent in 1993 to 16 per cent in 1994 – eight percentage points. The other three areas showed smaller changes, the largest being in Bournemouth which showed an increase of four percentage points (from 17% in 1993 to 21% in 1994).

Table 2.2 Offending on bail charge rates in 1993 and 1994 (sample sizes are given in brackets)

Court area	Percent charged with an offence committed while on COURT bail		Percent charged with an offence committed while on POLICE bail	
	1993	1994	1993	1994
Bournemouth	17% (178)	21% (226)	7% (243)	11% (446)
Horseferry Rd	22% (191)	16% (207)	12% (236)	10% (99)
Leicester	24% (485)	16% (439)	13% (809)	12% (767)
Newport	21% (132)	18% (131)	12% (467)	12% (480)
Salford	28% (185)	31% (175)	8% (171)	6% (80)
All areas	23%(1,171)	20%(1,178)	12%(1,926)	11%(1,872)

It is important to look further into how the changes came about. Chapter 5 of this report shows how the rates of offending on bail varied with the characteristics of the defendants granted bail. The factors found to be associated with higher rates of offending on bail include selected categories of current offence, homelessness, a previous criminal history and/or a previous history of breaches of bail, unemployment, younger age groups and longer waiting times before trial.

Some of these factors may reflect police targeting of known offenders so that those on bail are more likely to be caught when they reoffend. Changes in police practices regarding such targeting might also affect some of the comparisons but it is not possible to take this into acount in the analysis.

A reduction in offending on bail rates could have arisen in a variety of ways. The pattern of characteristics of those on bail might have changed as a result of changes elsewhere in the system, such as a greater use of cautions for younger defendants or a reduction in waiting times for trial. Or they might have changed because more defendants in the higher risk groups were remanded in custody. Alternatively, magistrates might have improved their targeting of defendants in the higher risk groups, thereby reducing offending on bail within these groups. It is therefore of interest to look not only at offending on bail rates overall, but also at the offending on bail rates within the higher risk groups, and at any changes in the custody rates.

Table 2.3 shows the remand decisions made at court in the five areas in 1993 and 1994. There were significant shifts in the pattern of decisions made both in Horseferry Road and in Leicester, but not in the other three areas.

Table 2.3 Court remand decisions in 1993 and 1994

Court area	Year	Uncond -itional bail	Conditional bail	Custody	Sample size
Bournemouth	1993	50%	34%	16%	292
	1994	58%	27%	15%	375
Horseferry Road	1993	58%	24%	18%	438
	1994	48%	28%	24%	468
Leicester	1993	60%	25%	15%	664
	1994	79%	11%	10%	657
Newport	1993	49%	34%	17%	272
	1994	50%	29%	21%	225
Salford	1993	53%	28%	19%	327
	1994	49%	33%	18%	237

Each area will be considered in turn to examine the changes made, the remand decisions and the consequent rates of offending on bail.

Bournemouth and Poole

The changes made in the Bournemouth and Poole court areas were as follows:

- Pre-court discussions: court listing times were changed to allow pre-court discussions to be scheduled for 9.40 am.

- Bail notices: these were issued to defendants given unconditional bail as well as those given bail with conditions. The notices require defendants to appear at court at least 15 minutes before the time their cases are listed.

- Bail conditions: the wording of conditions imposing residence or a curfew were changed to enable the police to ensure tighter enforcement.

- Training for magistrates and use of bail hostels: refresher training on the Bail Act was carried out. Also, a report was issued to magistrates which advised them of the need for breaches of bail conditions to be taken seriously, the appropriate response when defendants were known to have committed offences while on bail, and the need to consider the use of bail hostel places.

- Bail information scheme: a new scheme was started in Dorchester prison. A steering group mechanism was established for the court based and prison based scheme, to operate through the Court User Group. A procedure for handling negative information was agreed.

- A new bail support scheme was set up for 18- to 25-year-olds in part of the court area.

- Record of argument in bail decisions: any representations made during remand hearings were to be recorded by the court clerk.

The offending on court bail rate in Bournemouth stayed the same in 1993 and 1994 (at 16%). This remained the case when the pattern of characteristics in the two years was taken into account. The offending on bail rates for the high risk groups showed different patterns: some increased (the rate for those under 21 increased slightly from 23% in 1993 to 26% in 1994); some decreased (the rate for defendants who waited more than three months before trial decreased from 32% to 28%); and many stayed at about the same level.

It is interesting to note from Table 2.2 that the offending on bail *charge* rates increased by four percentage points between 1993 and 1994 for both court bail and police bail after charge. This indicates that fewer of those charged with offences on bail in 1994 were convicted of those offences than was the case in 1993.

In Bournemouth, there is some evidence of a shift between 1993 and 1994 from conditional bail to unconditional bail (of about eight percentage points), but the custody rates stayed about the same.

These results show that the projects had no clear effects on the levels of offending on bail in Bournemouth and Poole.

Horseferry Road

The changes made in the Horseferry Road area were as follows:

• Criminal records: the criminal records office agreed to provide a full record (i.e., the microfiche) in cases where formerly only a brief computerised record of the last three convictions had been available.

• Bail notices: these were issued to those given unconditional bail as well as those given bail with conditions.

• Information on bail decisions: the time taken for the results of bail hearings to be produced and passed to the police was reduced.

• Custody officer training: guidelines were produced for custody officers on the factors which magistrates typically consider in their remand decisions, the aim being to assist the officers in completing the form (MG7) which gives their recommendation to the CPS.

• Training for magistrates: police officers took part in the programme of magistrates' training.

• Record of bail decisions: any representations made during remand hearings were to be recorded by the court clerk.

Table 2.1 shows that the rate of offending on court bail decreased from 18 per cent in 1993 to 11 per cent in 1994. Part of this difference is accounted for by changes in the waiting time before trial and in the proportion of defendants who had previous custodial sentences in the Horseferry Road area. However, there were decreases in the offending on bail rates in 1994 for most high risk groups of defendants. For example, the rates for defendants with a previous custodial sentence and a previous bail history decreased from 27 per cent in 1993 to 10 per cent in 1994; the rate for defendants who were unemployed decreased from 23 per cent in 1993 to 12 per cent in 1994. The rate for defendants who waited more than three months before trial decreased from 30 per cent in 1993 to 20 per cent in 1994, and the rate for those who waited more than six months before trial decreased from 24 per cent in 1993 to 14 per cent in 1994. (The samples from Horseferry Road included very few youth defendants as the Inner London Youth Court was not included in the research.)

Remand decisions in Horseferry Road showed a shift from unconditional bail to conditional bail and custody. The conditional bail rate went up from 24 per cent in 1993 to 28 per cent in 1994 and the custody rate increased from 18 per cent to 24 per cent.

Although custody rates increased for most groups of defendants, the increases were higher than the average (of six percentage points) for the higher risk categories. For example, the custody rate for those charged with more serious offences[3] increased by 13 percentage points (from 47% to 60%); for those who had a previous bail history and had served a previous custodial sentence, the increase was nine percentage points; and for the unemployed, the increase was seven percentage points.

In summary, there was a clear reduction in the level of offending on bail by defendants in Horseferry Road and this was the result of more defendants in all groups, but specifically in the higher risk groups, being remanded in custody. It seems likely that this arose from the increased priority that was given to reducing the level of offending on bail in 1992/93.

Leicester

The changes made in the Leicester court area were as follows:

- Bail records: the police established mechanisms to ensure that, when a defendant appeared at court, the court was informed if he was already on bail from another police station or court in the force area.

- Bail notices: these were issued to defendants given unconditional bail as well as those given bail with conditions.

- Bail conditions: conditions imposing residence or a curfew required the defendant to present himself to any police officer who was checking on compliance. Monitoring exercises were carried out to assess the level of breaches of these conditions.

- Training for magistrates: all bench chairmen (about a third of the 300 magistrates) attended a training programme using the Bail Risk Exercise. Also, representatives from each agency (police custody officers, CPS, magistrates, probation officers, and court clerks and defence solicitors) took part in the seminars led by Professor Hassett, described in Chapter 3. The aim was to look at the approach of each agency to the assessment of risks of absconding and reoffending, and also at which factors were taken into account, and the relative importance of these.

---

3   Theses include burglary, robbery and the more serious violence, sex and drug offences.

- Bail information schemes: liaison was established between the court and prison based schemes.

- Record of argument in bail decisions: any representations made during remand hearings were to be recorded by the court clerk.

- Saturday courts: new arrangements were made for access to the Probation Service at Saturday courts.

Table 2.1 shows that the rate of offending on court bail in Leicester decreased from 20 per cent in 1993 to 12 per cent in 1994. When account was taken of changes in the pattern of characteristics of defendants and their offences between the two years, there was still a significant decrease in the offending on bail rate.

There were decreases in the offending on bail rates for most high risk groups of defendants in 1994. For example, the rates for defendants with a previous custodial sentence and a previous bail history decreased from 34 per cent in 1993 to 24 per cent in 1994; the rate for defendants who were unemployed decreased from 25 per cent in 1993 to 14 per cent in 1994. The rate for defendants who waited more than three months before trial decreased from 25 per cent in 1993 to 15 per cent in 1994, and the rate for those who waited more than six months before trial decreased from 35 per cent in 1993 to 22 per cent in 1994. Around 40 per cent of defendants in Leicester were aged under 21. Within this group, the offending on bail rates for those under 18 decreased from 36 per cent in 1993 to 18 per cent in 1994, and the rate for the 18- to 21-year-olds decreased from 25 per cent to 19 per cent.

The Leicester results show a different pattern from Horseferry Road in that the reduction in offending on bail rates *is not explained* by higher custody rates. On the contrary, there was a shift away from custody (from 15% in 1993 to 10% in 1994), and away from conditional bail (from 25% to 11%) towards more unconditional bail (from 60% in 1993 to 79% in 1994).

The decrease in custody rates was greater than average for younger defendants (10 percentage points for those under 18) and lower for those with a previous bail history who had also served a custodial sentence (three percentage points). For most other categories of defendant, the custody rates were lower in 1994 by around five percentage points.

In summary, the reduction in offending on bail in Leicester does not seem to have been caused by any shift in the pattern of defendant characteristics, or by more defendants being remanded in custody. It looks then, as though magistrates improved their skills in the assessment of risk, possibly as a result of the additional information that was provided by the police about defendants who were already on bail, or as a result of the extra training courses that were held.

Newport

The changes made in the Newport court area were as follows:

- Access to criminal records: 24 hour direct access to the local criminal records office was made available (to replace the limited 9am to 5pm access available previously).

- Bail conditions: a more stringent definition of the conditions imposing residence or a curfew were agreed.

- Training for custody officers: a two-day training course on bail decision-making was set up for custody officers.

- Training for magistrates: training was organised which drew on the Bail Risk Exercise.

- Appropriate adults: a scheme was established whereby volunteers would act as 'appropriate adults' to be present when those aged under 17 were interviewed by the police (the need for such volunteers arises when neither a parent, guardian or social worker is available).

- Three other initiatives (to introduce a bail information scheme at Cardiff prison, a remand fostering scheme, and a psychiatric referral/diversion scheme) were all delayed by lack of resources.

The offending on court bail rate in Newport changed little between 1993 and 1994 (18% and 17% respectively). This remained the case when the pattern of characteristics in the two years was taken into account. The offending on bail rates for the high risk groups showed different patterns, although some of these differences are likely to be the result of the small numbers of defendants in these groups. The rate for defendants aged under 21 increased, from 22 per cent in 1993 to 34 per cent in 1994 and so did the rate for those who waited more than three months before trial (from 27% to 39%). Some decreased, i.e. the rate for defendants who had served a previous custodial sentence and/or had a previous bail history decreased from 27 per cent to 22 per cent, while the rates for other groups stayed broadly the same.

Remand decisions in Newport showed a small shift between conditional bail and custody. The use of conditional bail decreased from 34 per cent in 1993 to 29 per cent in 1994, while the custody rate increased from 17 per cent to 21 per cent between these years. The unconditional bail rates stayed about the same.

It is interesting to note that the custody rates increased for those who had served a previous custodial sentence and/or had a previous bail history (from 25% in 1993 to 34% in 1994). This may have been the result of the improvement in the availability of criminal records in Newport in 1994, and could have caused the reduction in offending on bail rates for this group indicated above. In contrast, the custody rates for those aged under 21 did not change.

In summary, the project appeared to have no overall effect on offending on bail in Newport, but there seems to have been a reduction in offending on bail in some high risk groups which has been balanced out by increases in other groups.

Salford

The changes made in the Salford court area were as follows:

- Training for custody officers: a programme of training was implemented.

- Training for magistrates: four training sessions were organised on structured decision-making using the Bail Risk Exercise (125 out of 180 magistrates attended these). Also, a programme of visits to local bail hostels was arranged.

- Mentally disordered offenders: new arrangements were made for a review panel for the diversion of mentally disordered offenders. A probation officer took charge of this project, assisted by a community psychiatric nurse. Magistrates, clerks and other court users were briefed about the services that could be provided.

- Bail support: although attempts were made to set up a bail support scheme for young offenders in Salford, funding could not be arranged in time for the second phase of the project.

The offending on court bail rate in Salford increased slightly from 23% in 1993 to 25% in 1994. When the pattern of characteristics in the two years was taken into account, this small difference was not found to be significant.

The high rates of offending on bail in Salford compared with the other areas are partly explained by the characteristics of the defendants dealt with: there were the highest proportions of under-18-year-olds, 18- to 21-year-olds and unemployed defendants. The Salford sample also included the highest proportion of defendants who had served a previous custodial sentence or who had a previous history of bail breaches and, in 1994, included higher than average proportions of defendants waiting more than three months for trial.

The offending on bail rates for defendants in the higher risk groups either changed by small amounts or stayed the same. For example, the rate for the under-21-year-olds increased from 32 per cent in 1993 to 34 per cent in 1994; the rates for defendants who waited more than three months for trial decreased from 35 per cent in 1993 to 32 per cent in 1994; and the rates for defendants who had served a previous custodial sentence or who had a previous bail history decreased from 33 per cent to 31 per cent. The rates for the unemployed stayed the same in the two years.

The court remand decisions in Salford showed a shift from unconditional bail to conditional bail (of about four percentage points) between 1993 and 1994, whereas the custody rates stayed about the same.

In summary, the project seems to have had no clear effect on offending on bail rates in Salford.

Evaluation: magistrates' views on the deficiencies in information received

As part of the case tracking exercise,[4] magistrates were asked for their views on:

- whether the information they had been given in court was unreliable or otherwise deficient. If so, what this was

- whether they would have liked further information, and if so, what this was.

Unreliable or deficient information was recorded in 12 per cent of around 1,000 cases in 1993 and in 12 per cent of around 900 cases in 1994. Magistrates would have liked further information in eight per cent of these cases in both years.

---

4   This information was only collected in cases where there was some doubt that unconditional bail would be appropriate. The Justices' Clerks advised that, when all parties – police CPS and court – agreed that unconditional bail was appropriate, the cases would be dealt with very quickly at remand hearings: hence the completion of additional forms in the courts would have imposed too great a burden.

Table 2.4 Further information that magistrates wished to have

Information required	1993		1994	
	Times mentioned	Percentage of cases[1]	Times mentined	Percentage of cases[1]
More detail of current offence	38	38%	11	16%
Previous convictions	26	26%	26	37%
Confirmation of defendant's identity	5	5%	2	3%
Defendant's circumstances	5	5%	1	2%
Home address or temporary accommodation	8	8%	5	7%
Mental/medical state	4	4%	2	3%
Immigration status	2	2%	1	1%
Details of parallel charges	9	9%	3	6%
Offences taken into consideration (TICs)	2	2%	-	
Reasons for earlier remand decision (by police or court)	7	7%	5	7%
Behaviour on previous periods of bail	6	6%	3	4%
Possibility of bail hostel	-		3	4%
Availability of secure accommodation	-		2	3%
Others	3	3%	5	7%
Number of cases	100	(=100%)	70	(=100%)

Note 1: These are the percentages of cases in which specific items were mentioned.

Note 2: The percentages for 1993 add to more than 100 because more than one item of information was mentioned for some cases.

Table 2.4 shows the categories of information mentioned by magistrates as 'unreliable or otherwise deficient' or as 'further information required'. (The answers to these two questions have been combined because, in many cases, they contained the same points.) In some cases in 1993, more than one category of deficient or missing information was mentioned by the same bench : all such items are included in the table. In other cases, mainly in 1994, the fact that there had been deficient or missing information was recorded, but no details of this information were given: such cases are omitted from the table. This means that less detail is available about information deficiencies in the 1994 sample cases than is available for the 1993 cases (70 cases/items of information in 1994 compared with 100 cases/115 items of information in 1993).

The table shows that more detail about the current offence was required most frequently in 1993 (in 38% of cases in which details of missing information were recorded) and second most frequently in 1994 (in 16% of such cases). The difference between the years arose from one area (Newport) which contributed half of these cases in 1993 and none in 1994. It seems, therefore, that there was an improvement in Newport in 1994 as regards the details that magistrates were given of the current offence. In many of the cases studied, the magistrates said that the information they were given about the offence was sketchy or confusing. Other magistrates mentioned such items as: victims and their injuries – there was not sufficient detail; the sum of money involved in a fraud or a theft was not known; there was confusion between two cars involved in an offence; the sequence of events was unclear; there was not enough detail of other persons involved in the incident; or the date and time of the offence was not given.

The lack of previous conviction information was mentioned next most frequently in 1993 – in 26 per cent of the responses, and most frequently in 1994 – in 37 per cent of the responses. Several other categories of information were mentioned, the largest group relating to information concerning the defendant – his true identity, address or the need for accommodation, mental state, immigration status or other (undefined) circumstances. Together these headings arose in 24 per cent of cases in 1993 and 16 per cent in 1994.

Another category included information regarding offences, i.e., those taken into consideration or other charges that were being dealt with in parallel to the current charges. These were mentioned in 11 per cent of cases in 1993 and six per cent of cases in 1994.

Lack of information on previous remand decisions in the current proceedings or the defendant's behaviour on previous periods of bail were mentioned in 13 per cent of cases in 1993 and 11 per cent of cases in 1994. Information regarding the availability of a bail hostel or of secure accommodation was mentioned in seven per cent of cases in 1994 only (these arose in Bournemouth and Leicester courts).

Other miscellaneous items of missing information were mentioned in single cases. In many of these, the brief comment made on the form was not sufficient to describe the magistrates' problems. These items include the reason for the lack of a compensation claim, the likelihood of the prisoner being produced from prison, the requirements of the defendant while on parole licence, 'security information re the recent arrest', and the reason that the CPS file was not available.

Although the above figures show some small reductions in 1994, they are based on relatively small sample sizes (100 and 70), and do not, therefore, show changes which are statistically significant. The only clear change seems to have been in Newport, where there was an improvement in 1994 in the information that was given to magistrates regarding the current offence.

3 Bail/custody decisions: consulting the decision-makers

The exercises described in this section were held to explore with magistrates, first, the information they would like to have when they are making remand decisions and, second, how this information is used. The sessions were led by Professor Patricia Hassett of the University of Syracuse (New York State) and were carried out with the assistance of the authors.[1]

Leicester court volunteered to take part in the exercise as part of its commitment to improving the training of magistrates.[2] Nine experienced bench chairmen took part and, at their suggestion, the other agencies involved in pre-trial decisions were invited to take part also. Accordingly, the exercise was organised around eight groups:

• three groups of three magistrates (bench chairmen)

• one group of three custody officers

• one group of three CPS prosecutors

• one group of three defence solicitors

• one group of three court clerks

• one group of three probation officers.

Input was given from each group working together, rather than from individuals, to simulate the conditions that lay magistrates experience in court. The exercise consisted of three evening sessions each lasting about two hours.

---

1 Professor Hassett was engaged on commparative research on bail decisions in England and New York State, and the possible use of expert computer systems as aids to these decisions (Hassett, 1992, gives some early work on this topic).

2 As described in Chapter 2, all magistrates who were bench chairmen in the Leicester Division attended a one day course in remand decision-making in 1993/4. This course used the 'Bail Risk Exercise' prepared by the Magistrates' Association.

Design of the exercises

In the first session, each group was asked to consider one of the risks set out in the Bail Act, 1976, and to list what information it would need to make an assessment of this risk. The Bail Act requires magistrates to assess whether defendants are likely to:

(i)   fail to appear at court

(ii)   commit offences while they are on bail

(iii)   interfere with witnesses

Three groups considered the first risk, three the second risk and two the third risk. Seventy-five items of information were identified as relevant to risk (i), 99 items relevant to risk (ii) and 28 to risk (iii): there was considerable overlapping between these three sets. In order to focus on those items that were most important, and also were likely to be available, subsequent sessions involved hypothetical cases. These were derived from real cases, but were altered to give a balance of different factors. Only limited information was given. Each group of decision-makers was asked to assess one of the three main risks for each case, and to make a remand decision based on that risk alone. They were also asked to indicate:

• which pieces of information had contributed to their decision

• whether each had increased or decreased the risk they were considering

• why it increased or decreased the risk

• what the relative importance of each piece of information was.

To assess the relative importance of individual items of information, the groups were asked to assign 100 points between the factors in each decision: hence a very important fact might be given 50 points, whereas any that were not important would be given few or no points. Furthermore, the importance of a factor might either be in increasing the risk or in decreasing the risk.

Information identified as important in remand decisions and why

Some of the results of this exercise which relate to the risk of offending while on bail and absconding are shown in Tables 3.1 and 3.2.[3] Although they are based on the hypothetical cases, the aim was to draw from these some more general conclusions about the relationships between the facts of a case and the assessment of risk. In the tables, the factors are listed in the order of importance that was attached to them in the hypothetical cases (averaged over all these cases). (The cases are given in Appendix B.)

Considering first the risk of offending while on bail (Table 3.1), the important factors were judged to be the defendant's:

- criminal record

- current offence and the harm inflicted

- housing situation

- likely sentence if convicted

- substance abuse

- previous record while on bail

- employment status

- family ties

- community or criminal ties.

The most important factor was held to be the defendant's previous criminal record, and this was partly linked to the fourth factor, the likely sentence if convicted. The second column of Table 3.1 gives some of the possible alternatives that will apply in individual cases: there may be no criminal record, a short or not very serious record, or a long record. If the defendant has no criminal record, he was judged to be a lower risk because he was less likely to get a custodial sentence and hence, from factor 4, to have more to lose by committing more offences. If he has a record but not a very serious one, the effect on risk would be variable: the record may increase the risk of

---

3   The hypothetical cases did not provide sufficient information relevant to the risk of interference with witnesses so this was excluded.

a custodial sentence, and this again, from factor 4, may suggest that he has nothing to lose by committing more offences. The third possibility is that he may have a long criminal record – in which case he was regarded as a higher risk because he might be likely to get a custodial sentence (as before). Also, the risk of reoffending was judged to be higher because the pattern of offending may well continue, particularly if he has committed a series of similar offences in the past.

The factor judged second in importance was the current offence. An offence which resulted in a significant amount of harm to a victim would cause the defendant to be judged a higher risk, again, because it might make him more likely to get a custodial sentence and hence he would have little to lose by offending while on bail. An offence which caused little harm was judged to have no clear effect on the risk.

Considering the risk of failing to appear at court (Table 3.2), the most important factors were judged to be:

- likely sentence if convicted

- current offence and the harm inflicted

- housing situation

- family ties

- criminal record (related to likely sentence)

- previous record while on bail

- employment status

- substance abuse.

Regarding the first of these factors, if a custodial sentence is unlikely, the risk of absconding was judged to be lower. If a custodial sentence (or a heavy fine to a person of limited means) is likely, the defendant would be more likely to fail to appear at court to avoid it.

It is clear that some of the factors listed are interlinked, e.g., the current offence, criminal record and likely sentence. This apparent duplication might have arisen from the artificial nature of the exercise. Groups were asked to mark the factors which were relevant to each case on a list of around 100, some of which were overlapping, which were taken from the lists compiled in the first session. The effect may have been to inflate the number of factors included.

It will also be noted that the same factors (apart from community or criminal ties) appear in both Tables 3.1 and 3.2, although they appear in a different order of priority in each table. This suggests that, when they make a remand decision, decision-makers do not separate out the risk of failing to appear from the risk of reoffending, but rather make a judgement of the risk of whether either is likely. The discussion during the exercise reinforced this suggestion. (The Bail Risk Exercise involves making a separate assessment of each risk.)

Another point that emerged in discussion concerned the importance to decision-makers of the current offence. It was felt that the decision to grant or withhold bail was not only based on the risk of offending on bail (say) but also on a judgement of the harm that such offending would do. Hence, a person who was assessed as a high risk of offending on bail, on the basis of his previous offending history, would be unlikely to be remanded in custody if the current offence was a minor one (e.g. theft of low value goods). Whereas, a defendant who was judged to be a lower risk, but had committed a violent offence (say GBH), would be much more likely to be remanded in custody because any further offences would put the public at a greater risk.

Another point that arose was the scarcity of available material on which magistrates and other decision-makers can base their assessments of risk. In most areas of activity, predictions of the future are based on analysis of past events. Hence if magistrates had regular feedback on the behaviour of defendants who had been granted bail, they would be in a better position to refine their decision-making over time. The lack of sufficient historical data regarding offending on bail arises partly because of the sheer difficulty, and hence the expense, of following up offenders to record their behaviour on bail, and partly because the results of such research in the past have not been conclusive, i.e., it has not been possible to distinguish which groups of offenders are high bail risks. Chapter 5 of this report gives some results on this topic from the case tracking data.

Table 3.1 Decision-makers' assessment of the relationship between the facts of the case and the risk of offending on bail (factors listed in descending order of importance)

Factor	Alternatives	Impact on Risk	Reason
1. Criminal record	No record	Decreases risk	Decreases risk of custodial sentence
	A few previous convictions	Uncertain impact	Might increase risk of custodial sentence
	Recidivist	Increases risk	If he has committed a series of similar offences, may well continue to offend
2. Current offence - harm inflicted	Trivial physical or financial harm	Uncertain impact	Will affect the sentence given (see 4.below)
	Significant physical or financial harm	Increases risk	Increases risk of a custodial sentence
3. Housing situation	Owner occupier or rents	Decreases risk	Has more to lose by offending
	Housing/hostel available	Uncertain impact	– – – –
	Homeless	Increases risk	May offend to provide food and shelter
4. Likely sentence if convicted	Likely non-custodial	Decreases risk	Reoffending may attract heavier sentence
	Short custodial	Uncertain impact	– – – –
	Long custodial	Increases risk	Nothing to lose by further offences
5. Substance abuse	No problems	Uncertain impact	– – – –
	Drug or alcohol abuse	Increases risk	May continue to offend to finance supply of drugs or alcohol

Table 3.1 cont'd

Factor	Alternatives	Impact on Risk	Reason
6. Previous record while on bail	Has been on bail before and has not offended	Decreases risk	Past behaviour is likely to be a good predictor of future behaviour
	Offences have been committed while on bail	Increases risk	
7. Employment status	Long term employment	Decreases risk	Likely to be more stable: more to lose by further offending
	Occasional employment	Uncertain impact	- - - -
	No job	Increases risk	Has less to lose by reoffending
8. Family ties	Stable family ties for a length of time	Decreases risk	May give support and prevent offending
	No family ties or previous offending despite family ties	Uncertain impact	- - - -
	Unsupportive family	Increases risk	Nothing to lose by offending
9. Community ties or criminal ties	Good community ties but no criminal ties	Decreases risk	No obvious influence to reoffend
	No ties of any sort	Uncertain impact	- - - -
	Criminal associates	Increases risk	May draw him into further crime

Table 3.2 Decision-makers' assessment of the relationship between the facts of the case and the risk of failing to appear at court (factors listed in descending order of importance)

Factor	Alternatives	Impact on Risk	Reason
1. Likely sentence if convicted	Custodial sentence or heavy fine unlikely	Decreases risk	Less reason to fail to appear to avoid sentence
	Custodial sentence likely OR heavy fine likely and has limited means	Increases risk to avoid custodial sentence or heavy fine	May fail to appear
2. Nature of crime	Physical or financial harm not significant	Uncertain impact	- - - -
	Significant injuries caused/weapons used/or significant financial gain	Increases risk	More likely to get custodial sentence (see 1.)
3. Housing situation	Owns or rents a home or lives with parent	Decreases risk	Can be contacted if s/he fails to appear
	No fixed abode	Increases risk	No means of contact if fails to appear
4. Family ties	Has dependent partner or children or supportive partner	Decreases risk	Family support may have good influence on behaviour. Defendant has more to lose by failing to appear or leaving the area
	Has no family ties	Increases risk	Has less to lose by leaving the area and failing to appear
5. Criminal record	No previous record	Decreases risk	Less likely to get custodial sentence (see 1.)
	Has record of similar offences	Increases risk	More likely to get custodial sentence (see 1.)

Table 3.2 cont'd

Factor	Alternatives	Impact on Risk	Reason
6. Previous record while on bail	Has always appeared before	Decreases risk	Past behaviour is likely to be a good predictor of future behaviour
	No bail record or record not known	Uncertain impact	
	Failed to appear on previous bail	Increases risk	
7. Employment status	In steady employment	Decreases risk	Has more to lose by failure to appear or leaving the area
	Unemployed	Increases risk	Has less to lose by failure to appear or leaving the area
8. Substance abuse	No known problems	Uncertain impact	----
	Alcohol or drug abuse	Increases risk	The effect of the alcohol or drugs is likely to make behaviour less predictable and appointments may be broken

4 Bail/custody decisions and the factors that affect them

Magistrates' remand decisions are based partly on the recommendations made by other agencies (the Crown Prosecution Service, the police and the defence), and partly on the information they are given about the defendants and their offences. This chapter looks first at the extent to which the decisions made agreed with the recommendations, and then at the extent to which they are associated with specific characteristics of the defendant. These two aspects are not mutually exclusive, since the recommendations made by the police and Crown Prosecution Service (CPS) will have been based on the characteristics of the defendant.

Links between decisions by different agencies

The case tracking data collected in 1993 and 1994 were analysed to show the extent of agreement or otherwise between the police, the CPS and the magistrates on the bail/custody decisions made. Figure 4.1 shows the decisions made by the police, CPS and courts in the samples. The relationship between the police decisions and the CPS recommendation was examined first. When the police had granted bail before the first court appearance, the prosecutors had no objection[1] to unconditional bail being granted by the court in the vast majority of cases (92%). A small percentage (7%) were granted conditional bail and one per cent were remanded in custody.

There was not so much agreement when the police had held the defendant in custody before the first court appearance: the CPS recommended that 46 per cent of those held in custody by the police should be granted bail with conditions, and that 48 per cent should be held in custody. A reason for this is that, prior to 1995, the police did not have the power to attach conditions to bail. Hence, in many cases, they would hold a person in custody and recommend that the court should attach conditions to bail. More surprising is the CPS recommendation of unconditional bail for six per cent of the police custody cases.

---

1   Under the Bail Act, 1976, there is a presumption of (unconditional) bail. Hence, if the CPS wish to recommend bail with conditions or remand in custody, their recommendation takes the form of an 'objection' to bail

Looking next at the relationship between the CPS recommendations and the court decisions, it is clear that, again, there was a high degree of agreement on unconditional bail. When the CPS had no objection to bail, the court granted it in 99 per cent[2] of cases. When the prosecutor recommended bail with conditions, the court agreed in 89 per cent[3] of cases. The least agreement was found when the prosecutor recommended custody: the court agreed in 75 per cent of cases, and granted bail, mostly with conditions, in 25 per cent. It is likely that this shift from custody to bail arose from defence lawyers' submissions in favour of bail: there was such a submission in nearly half of the cases. In 12 of the 169 cases in which conditional bail was granted, bail information was provided, and in three of these, accommodation was offered.[4] Magistrates recorded, in a few cases, that the offence was not sufficiently serious to warrant a custodial remand.[5]

All parties agreed that unconditional bail was appropriate in a large group of cases (1,945 or 53% of the total). The volume of such cases[6] was pointed out by the agencies when the case tracking exercise was planned. There was concern that a need for the CPS and the courts to record details would cause delay to the proceedings. In consequence, it was agreed that fewer details of the decisions made in these cases would be recorded. (Details of the defendants and charges were obtained from standard police forms.)

---

2   This is calculated from two branches of Figure 4.1, i.e. (1945+84) / (1958+93) = .99.

3   This is calculated from two branches of Figure 4.1, i.e. (122+635) / (141+707) = .89.

4   Bail information would not have been produced in the 7 cases in which the defendant had been granted police bail.

5   Although magistrates were asked to record the reason for their decision, in most of these cases, they gave the reasons why they did not grant unconditional bail rather than the reason why they disagreed with the CPS recommendation for custody.

6   These cases will be called the 'agreed bail' cases.

Figure 4.1 Decision tree of remand decisions – persons remanded by the courts in 5 areas in 93 and 94

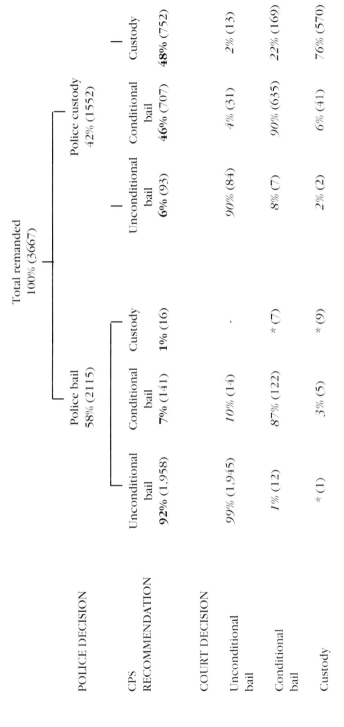

Police bail/custody decision – related factors

Since the police bail/custody decision clearly influences the later decisions made by the court, it is interesting to see how it is related to the characteristics of the defendant and the offence.[7]

Analysis showed that factors which were associated with the highest custody rates after charge were:

- address status – no fixed abode (90% of 250 defendants were held in custody)

- charged with failure to appear at court (88% of 137 defendants were held in custody)[8]

- known to have breached bail in the past (59% of 688 defendants were held in custody)

- currently on bail (51% of 916 defendants were held in custody)

- unemployed (34% of 3,842 defendants were held in custody).

The police custody rates for the five areas were as follows: Bournemouth – 32 per cent, Horseferry Road – 33 per cent, Leicester – 25 per cent, Newport – 20 per cent and Salford – 51 per cent (for 1993 and 1994 together). Although analysis showed that most of these differences can be explained by differences in the defendant characteristics, Salford was shown to be high compared with the other areas. These high rates at Salford are partly explained by the large number of cases in which bail was breached in the area[9].

Court bail/custody decisions – related factors

Analyses of nearly 4,000 court remand decisions suggested that the factors which had the most bearing on the decision were:

- address status (whether the defendant was homeless or not)

---

7   Earlier research on police and court remand decisions in relation to defendants' characteristics was described by Morgan and Pearce (1989).

8   Most of these defendants are likely to have been arrested on bench warrants not backed for bail. Hence the custody decisions were really made by the court.

9   There was some under-recording of the police data in Salford, particularly in 1994, and some evidence to suggest that the missing cases were those that had been given bail. The multivariate analysis took account of this, by relating the bail decisions to the defendant characteristics, but still showed a higher custody rate for Salford than for the other four areas.

- the type of offence currently charged (grouped into 'more serious' and 'less serious')[10]

- bail history (any previous instances of absconding or breaching bail conditions, or whether the defendant was already on bail when charged with the current offence)

- whether the defendant had served a custodial sentence (this appeared to be the most important aspect of the criminal record)

- employment status

- gender (a marginal effect only).

Table 4.1 shows how these factors were related to the custody rates. (Age has been included in the table for interest although it was not found to affect the decision in a consistent way.) The rate varied from two per cent to five per cent of defendants who were charged with 'less serious' offences, had no bail history and had not served a custodial sentence in the past, to 64 per cent for persons charged with 'more serious' offences and had no fixed address. Although this table shows some very high figures for persons remanded in custody, these are mainly for small groups of defendants. More than half of the defendants studied fell into the category of 'no previous custodial sentence and no previous bail history', and around four-fifths of these were charged with less serious offences. This last group had the lowest custody rates of two per cent to five per cent, i.e. they include defendants regarded as the lowest risks.

---

10   The category 'more serious' offences was defined from the results of preliminary data analyses to include those offences which attracted higher custody rates. These were burglary, robbery, GBH, indictable/either-way sex offences and drug trafficking. All other were categorised as 'less serious' offences.

Table 4.1 Court decisions: custody rates for combinations of defendant characteristics

Factor	More serious offences[10]		Less serious offences[10]	
No fixed address	64%	(90)	37%	(148)
Has a home address				
Has both a previous custodial sentence and a bail history				
Unemployed	58%	(144)	25%	(334)
Employed	54%	(13)	26%	(38)
Males	58%	(156)	26%	(358)
Females	---	---	15%	(20)
Aged under 21	56%	(48)	35%	(77)
Aged 21 or over	59%	(109)	23%	(300)
Either a previous custodial sentence or a bail history				
Unemployed	44%	(207)	14%	(580)
Employed	22%	(55)	7%	(215)
Males	40%	(255)	14%	(697)
Females	22%	(9)	6%	(105)
Aged under 21	41%	(276)	15%	(276)
Aged 21 or over	39%	(149)	12%	(504)
Neither a previous custodial sentence nor a bail history				
Unemployed	22%	(18)	5%	(814)
Employed	16%	(156)	2%	(768)
Males	20%	(332)	4%	(1,355)
Females	11%	(19)	2%	(252)
Aged under 21	13%	(142)	2%	(422)
Aged 21 or over	24%	(203)	5%	(1,137)

The court custody rates (1993 and 1994 combined) for the five areas were as follows: Bournemouth and Poole – 16 per cent, Horseferry Road – 21 per cent, Leicester – 13 per cent, Newport – 19 per cent and Salford – 18 per cent. However, when the different balance of defendant characteristics in the areas was taken into account, analysis showed that only Horseferry Road was significantly different from the other areas (the rate was marginally higher).

Court remand decisions and offending while on bail

Table 4.2 shows the link between the court remand decisions and the rates of offending on court bail.[11] It shows that, in 1,116 cases in which all agencies agreed on unconditional bail, 14 per cent were found to have committed offences while on bail. In the 320 cases where there was some doubt about bail but unconditional bail was granted, a slightly higher proportion of 17 per cent offended on bail. When conditional bail was granted (in 632 cases), 19 per cent offended on bail. And in 96 cases where the defendant was remanded in custody at the first hearing, but was subsequently granted bail, 38 per cent offended on bail.

Table 4.2 Court decision at first hearing and offending on bail

Factor rate	Remand decision	Offending on bail
'Agreed bail' cases	Unconditional bail	14% (1,116)
Not 'agreed bail' cases	Unconditional bail	17% (320)
	Conditional bail	19% (632)
	Custody	38% (96)

Note: the sample sizes are in given in brackets.

It was also possible to look at the link between the CPS recommendations and the rates of offending on bail. These rates are slightly lower but very similar to the rates in Table 4.2. Of those defendants for whom the CPS recommended:

- unconditional bail   – 13 per cent offended on bail (this includes the 'agreed bail' group);

- conditional bail   – 20 per cent offended on bail;

- custody   – 31 per cent offended on bail.

---

11   That is, the proportion of defendants found guilty of the original offence who were convicted of an offence commited while on bail.

It seems that the CPS recommendations were more cautious than the court decisions. This is to be expected, as the CPS prosecutors do not take account of the representations made by the defence.

Conditions attached to bail

There is some interest in bail conditions and their effectiveness. Table 4.3 shows the pattern of decisions that were imposed by the courts in all areas in 1994.

Table 4.3 Conditions attached to court bail : percentage of defendants given each condition

Condition	Percentage of defendants given condition
Residence	72%
Not to contact X	41%
Not to approach Y	28%
Curfew	20%
Report to police	18%
Surety	6%
Surrender passport	3%
Number of defendants	313

Note: the percentages add to more than 100 because more than one condition was often imposed on a defendant.

This table shows a similar pattern to that found by other research (Raine and Willson, 1994). Residence was the most commonly found condition and was often imposed together with others, such as a curfew. The next most common were restrictions on movements, usually to prevent the defendant approaching a victim, or to keep him away from places and contacts which may cause him to reoffend. A curfew was imposed on a fifth of defendants and just under a fifth were required to report to the police.

5 Who offended on bail

An important reason for carrying out research into offending on bail is to assist magistrates in their assessment of risk. The aim is to identify which defendants are likely to be poor bail risks by studying characteristics of those who were granted bail and who committed offences while they were on bail. In this chapter, the case tracking data collected as part of the Bail Process Project is used for this purpose. No distinction is made between the 1993 and 1994 cases so that larger samples are obtained and hence the inter-relationships of several characteristics can be studied.

Method used

As described in Chapter 2, the five police forces who took part in the Bail Process Project recorded details of the bail/custody decision made for each defendant charged with an imprisonable offence during three months of 1993 and three months of 1994. The appropriate CPS branches and magistrates' courts recorded their recommendation/decisions on bail or custody for the same defendants until either the defendant was dealt with, or a second court hearing had been held, whichever was the earlier: the recording forms were then returned to the Home Office. From these records, it was possible to select defendants who were given police bail after charge, or given court bail at the first hearing, or remanded in custody at the first hearing and given court bail at the second hearing.[1]

The date on which the case was finally dealt with (and hence the end of any period on court bail) was not recorded. The reasons for the termination of the recording after the second hearing were, first, to limit the extra work imposed on the CPS and courts to manageable proportions, and also to ensure that details of all cases were returned within a reasonable period after the end of the three months.

In 1995 and early 1996, researchers searched the criminal records at the National Identification Service at Scotland Yard (NIS) for, first, the dates on which the cases were finally dealt with by the courts and, second, for details

---

1   The courts advised that, in the majority of 'mixed remand' cases (in which there is a grant of bail after a remand in custody), the bail is granted at the second court hearing (sometimes, a full bail application is not made until this hearing). Although bail is granted at a later stage in some cases, it was not possible to include these cases in the study.

of any offences that were committed during the time the defendants were on police or court bail. This method had an important consequence for the measures of offending on bail that were used. Appendix C gives more details. It is sufficient to say here that the measure of offending on court bail in this study is based on defendants who were *found guilty* of the offence for which bail was granted[2] (which meant that the date of conviction/sentence could be found on the criminal record) unlike the measure used in the earlier Home Office and the Metropolitan Police research (see footnote 1 of Chapter 1). In the earlier studies, *all* defendants who were given bail in the selected cases were followed up for offending on bail. This problem did not apply to offending while on police bail.

Offending on bail rates in 1993 and 1994

Table 5.1 shows the proportions of defendants granted bail by the court in the five areas who were charged with an offence allegedly committed while they were on bail, and the proportion who were found guilty of such an offence. Out of more than 2,300 defendants granted bail by the five courts who were followed up at NIS, 21 per cent were charged with an offence and 17 per cent were found guilty of such an offence. Out of nearly 4,000 defendants granted bail after charge by the police in the five areas who were followed up at NIS, 11 per cent were charged with an offence and 9 per cent were found guilty of such an offence.

Table 5.1 Police and court bail: rates of offending on bail in 1993 and 1994

	Court bail	Police bail
Percentage granted bail who were *charged* with an offence committed while on bail	21%	11%
Percentage granted bail who were *convicted* of an offence committed while on bail	17%	9%
Number of defendants	2,343	3,798

The rest of this chapter will be concerned with convictions only. The term 'offending on bail' will be used as a shorthand for 'found guilty of at least one offence committed while on bail'.

---

2   Or, were found guilty of an amended charge in the same proceedings.

Court bail: offending rates and related factors

Statistical analyses have identified the factors that were most highly related to the rates of offending on bail. Table 5.2 shows these factors, taken one at a time, and the corresponding offending on bail rates.

The factor which was shown to be most important in explaining the offending on bail rates was the waiting time between first court appearance and trial or sentence: the offending on bail rate increased with this waiting time. (In most cases, this will have been the length of time that the defendants were on court bail. However, some defendants will have spent part of this period in custody.)

Amongst the factors shown to be important, the highest offending on bail rates were found for:

- persons with no fixed abode (42% offended on bail), although the number of such defendants was small (only 97 defendants or 4% of the whole sample)

- those who waited more than six months before trial or sentence (32% offended on bail)

- those charged with theft of cars or unauthorised taking (32%), burglary (29%), or robbery (23%)

- those with at least one previous breach of bail (27%), i.e., they had failed to appear at court in the past, had breached bail conditions in the past, or were on bail when charged with the current offence

- those who had served a previous custodial sentence (28%)

- those under 18 (29%)

- those who were unemployed or were not in the workforce (i.e., at school, retired etc.) (21%).

The lowest rates of offending on bail were found for:

- persons who waited less than one month before trial or sentence (4%)

- those who were employed (7%)

- those charged with sex offences (6%), assault (7%) or fraud (8%).

Table 5.2 Court bail: factors associated with higher/lower rates of offending on bail

Factor		Percentage who offended on bail	Number in category
Address status	No fixed abode	42%	97
	Had address	16%	2,246
Charged with:	Car theft	32%	157
	Burglary	29%	284
	Robbery	23%	57
	Theft	20%	545
	Fraud	8%	204
	Assault	7%	392
	Sex	6%	33
Age	17 and under	29%	373
	18–20	24%	411
	21 and over	13%	1,549
Criminal record	Had served a previous custodial sentence	28%	529
	None known	14%	1,762
Previous bail history	Had record of breaches	27%	781
	None known	12%	1,510
Employment status	Unemployed	21%	1,690
	Employed	7%	564
Waiting time	Over 6 months	32%	419
	Over 3 and up to 6 months	24%	620
	Over 2 and up to 3 months	17%	348
	Over 1 and up to 2 months	10%	517
	Up to 1 month	4%	439

Table 5.3 shows the offending on bail rates for combinations of the factors that are shown to be related to higher or lower rates of offending on bail. The number in brackets after each percentage gives the number of defendants on which the percentage is based. Hence, there were 32 defendants who had no fixed abode and who were charged with the offences of burglary, robbery or car theft. Of these, nearly two-thirds (63%) offended on bail. This is the highest rate of offending on bail found in the study and is the only one that is greater than 50 per cent. Sixty-five defendants had no fixed abode and were charged with offences other than burglary, robbery or car theft. Of these, about one-third offended while on bail.

Of those who had an address, the highest rates of offending were found for those who had a previous bail history, had served a previous custodial sentence, and who were charged with burglary, robbery or car theft. Of the 73 persons who fell into this category, 44 per cent offended on bail.

The lowest rates of offending on bail were found for defendants who had a fixed address, who had no previous bail history and who had not served a custodial sentence, and who were charged with offences other than burglary, robbery or car theft: the offending on bail rate was six per cent for the 760 adult defendants who met these criteria, and four per cent for the 357 employed defendants who met these criteria.

Some of the rates quoted in the table are very high (63% and 44%), but these apply to small groups of defendants. Just over a fifth of the defendants studied fell into groups with offending on bail rates of 25 per cent or higher; nearly half of the defendants fell into groups with offending on bail rates between 11 per cent and 25 per cent, and around a third fell into the group with an offending rate of six per cent or less.

The problem that magistrates face is how to target those defendants who will offend on bail from the groups shown. When the offending rate is as high as 44 per cent, the probability that these defendants will offend on bail is roughly the same as the probability that they will not so offend. An offending rate of six per cent means that there is a chance of around one in 16 that the defendants will offend on bail. It may be that other detail available (e.g., of the circumstances of the current offence and the pattern of previous convictions)[3] will make it possible for magistrates to refine their decisions within the categories given, or it may be that there is a degree of randomness in offending on bail which it is extremely difficult to predict.

---

3   The case tracking data did include some information on community and family ties, but this was not found to have a significant effect on the rate of offending on bail.

Table 5.3 Court bail: offending on bail rates for combinations of defendant characteristics

Factor	Burglary, robbery or car theft		Other charges	
No fixed address	63%	(32)	32%	(65)
Has a home address				
Has both a previous custodial sentence and a bail history				
Unemployed	44%	(69)	27%	(182)
Employed	50%	(4)	17%	(23)
Aged under 21	44%	(27)	39%	(31)
Aged 21 or over	44%	(46)	23%	(180)
Either a previous custodial sentence or a bail history				
Unemployed	33%	(139)	21%	(389)
Employed	12%	(17)	11%	(105)
Aged under 21	40%	(94)	28%	(174)
Aged 21 or over	17%	(64)	13%	(328)
Neither a previous custodial sentence nor a bail history				
Unemployed	21%	(176)	11%	(640)
Employed	4%	(47)	4%	(357)
Aged under 21	21%	(141)	16%	(295)
Aged 21 or over	17%	(97)	6%	(760)

Comparison of Table 5.3 with Table 4.1 shows some similarities in the composition of the groups that have high offending on bail rates (in Table 5.3) with the groups that have high custody rates (in Table 4.1). This suggests that the groups with high offending on bail rates attract high rates of remand in custody and, hence, are being targeted by magistrates. There are some differences in the offence categories in the two tables. The 'more serious' offences, which attract higher custody rates in Table 4.1, include the more serious sex and violence offences in addition to burglary, robbery and car theft: these last show high offending on bail rates in Table 5.3.

The reason for this is suggested by Chapter 3 in that magistrates take account of the risk to the public that would result from similar offences being committed while on bail. Hence, although persons charged with sex and violence offences are less likely to offend on bail, if they did so offend, there would be greater danger to the public.

Court bail: factors not related to the offending rates

Area. The offending on court bail rates for the five areas were: Bournemouth – 16 per cent, Horseferry Road – 15 per cent, Leicester – 17 per cent, Newport – 18 per cent, Salford – 24 per cent. However, when account was taken of the factors listed above, the difference between the five areas was not found to be statistically significant. Put another way, the area differences could be explained by the characteristics of the defendants in those areas. For example, the high rate at Salford arose from: a high proportion of the sample were under 18 (28% in Salford compared with 16% overall); a high proportion were unemployed (86% compared with 75% overall); and a high proportion had served a previous custodial sentence and had a bail history (19% compared with 13% overall). In comparison, the Horseferry Road sample included much smaller proportions of under 18s (2%)[4]; smaller proportions of unemployed (69%) and persons charged with burglary, robbery or car theft (10% compared with 22% overall).

Gender. Although there appeared to be a small difference between the offending on bail rates for males (18%) and females (15%), this was not statistically significant. (Females constituted 11% of the sample of 2,340.)

Court bail: offending rates and waiting time on bail

A possible way of reducing the rates of offending on bail is by reducing the time that defendants wait on bail before trial or sentence: this time is a characteristic of the system rather than of the defendant. Table 5.4 shows how the offending on bail rates increase with this waiting time, and also how the rates of increase differ according to other characteristics of the defendants. Defendants charged with burglary, robbery or car theft showed offending rates which increased from eight per cent for those who waited one month or less to 49 per cent for those who waited for more than six months, whereas the rates for defendants charged with other offences increased from three per cent to 23 per cent for the same waiting time periods. Previous record is also seen to be important. Defendants who had served a previous custodial sentence and had a history of breaching bail showed the sharpest increases: from six per cent for those who waited one

---

4   There was no recording at the Inner London Youth Courts.

month or less to 45 per cent for those who waited over six months. In contrast, defendants who had neither served a custodial sentence nor had previously breached bail, showed offending rates which varied from three per cent to 22 per cent over the same periods.

Table 5.4 Court bail: offending on bail rates for waiting times and other factors *(defendants who had a home address only)*

Offences charged	Burglary, robbery or car theft		Other charges	
Waiting time for trial / sentence				
Over 6 months	49%	(109)	23%	(295)
Over 3 and up to 6 months	31%	(131)	19%	(445)
Over 2 and up to 3 months	20%	(69)	15%	(267)
Over 1 and up to 2 months	15%	(95)	8%	(397)
Up to 1 month	8%	(65)	3%	(364)
All time periods	27%	(469)	14%	(1,768)

Previous record	Custodial sentence AND bail history		Custodial sentence OR bail history	Neither
Waiting time for trial / sentence				
Over 6 months	45%	(58)	37% (126)	22% (220)
Over 3 and up to 6 months	32%	(81)	31% (181)	14% (319)
Over 2 and up to 3 months	31%	(48)	22% (101)	10% (189)
Over 1 and up to 2 months	27%	(63)	8% (142)	6% (288)
Up to 1 month	6%	(34)	4% (114)	3% (282)
All time periods	30%	(284)	22% (664)	11% (1,298)

Using the data in Table 5.4, it is possible to estimate the possible effects on offending on bail of specific reductions in waiting time for trial. Arbitrary assumptions that might be made are that:

- waiting times of one month or less remain the same

- waiting times between one and six months are decreased by a month

- half of those who waited more than six months are dealt with in three to six months

- the offending on bail rates for each time period for the categories given in Table 5.4 remain the same.

Under these assumptions, the likely offending on bail rates for those charged with burglary etc., would be reduced from 27 per cent to 22 per cent, and for those charged with other offences from 14 per cent to 10 per cent. For both categories together, the likely reduction would be from 16 per cent to 13 per cent.

Similarly, for defendants who had served a custodial sentence *and* had breached bail, the likely reduction in offending on bail rates would be from 30 per cent to 24 per cent; for defendants who had either served a custodial sentence *or* had breached bail, the reduction would be from 22 per cent to 17 per cent; and for defendants with neither type of record, the likely reduction would be from 11 per cent to 8 per cent. Combining these three categories together, the likely reduction overall would be from 16 per cent to 13 per cent, which agrees with the results of the calculation above for offence categories.

Police bail after charge: offending rates and related factors

Nearly 3,800 defendants who had been granted bail by the police after charge were successfully followed up at NIS.[5] Unfortunately, information regarding criminal records, previous bail history and employment status was only available for 1,280 of these cases (i.e. those for which there was a court remand also, as these items were collected from the CPS recording forms). The relationships between the individual factors, considered separately, and the offending on police bail rates are given in Table 5.5. The highest rates were found for:

- those with no fixed abode (19% offended on police bail after charge)

- those aged under 18 (18%)

- those charged with robbery (18%) or car theft (15%)

---

5   This number is around 60% larger than the corresponding numbers given above for court bail. There are three reasons. First, the cases include many defendants who were dealt with by the court on first appearance; they include defendants for whom a police form was completed but not a CPS form (although every attempt was made to fill in the gaps); and they include defendants who were granted police bail regardless of whether they were found guilty (as the dates which defined the period of bail were recorded by the police – see Appendix C).

- those who had served a previous custodial sentence (14%)

- those who had a previous bail history (14%)

- the unemployed (14%)

- those who waited more than six weeks (13%).

The lowest rates of offending on police bail after charge were found for:

- those who waited less than three weeks (3%)

- those in employment (5%)

- those charged with assault or drug offences (5%) or fraud (6%)

- those aged 21 and over (6%)

- those with no previous breaches of bail (6%).

The area rates for offending on police bail were: Bournemouth – 7%, Horseferry Road – 10 per cent, Leicester – 10 per cent, Newport – 9 per cent and Salford – 6 per cent. Analysis showed that, when account was taken of the defendant characteristics in the five areas,[6] only Salford had a significantly different rate of offending on police bail: it was lower than the other areas.

---

6 Only those factors that had been recorded for the larger numbers of defendants were included, i.e. address status, age, current charge and gender.

Table 5.5 Police bail after charge: factors associated with higher/lower than average rates of offending while on bail

Factor	Percentage who offended on bail	Number in category
Address status		
No fixed abode	19%	27
Had address	9%	3,582
Age		
Under 18	18%	565
18–20	11%	681
21 and over	6%	2,533
Time on bail		
Over six weeks	13%	292
Over three and up to six weeks	9%	3,265
Up to three weeks	3%	233
Charged with:		
Robbery	18%	38
Car theft	15%	228
Burglary	12%	378
Theft	11%	1,027
Serious motoring	7%	416
Fraud	6%	329
Drug offences	5%	179
Assault	5%	416
Employment status[1]		
Unemployed	14%	920
Employed	5%	304
Previous bail history[1]		
Had record of breaches	14%	399
None known	6%	1,034
Criminal record[1]		
Had served a previous custodial sentence	14%	310
None known	7%	1,123

Note 1: Information was only available for part of the sample.

What offences are committed on bail?

A major concern of magistrates was found to be the seriousness of the offences committed while on bail and hence the danger that such offences will present to the public (see Chapter 3). The relationship between the original charge (the offence for which bail was granted) and any offences committed on bail is therefore of interest. For example, it is helpful to know if defendants charged with burglary or car theft commit more burglaries or car thefts while they are on bail

Table 5.6 gives a breakdown of 405 persons in the case tracking samples who offended on court bail by the original offence charged and the offence committed on bail. (Where there was more than one charge, an arbitrary order of seriousness was used to choose the most serious:[7] where more than one offence was committed on bail, the first such offence was chosen.) The table shows that there was most specialisation amongst those initially charged with burglary or theft (not of cars), of whom around half committed a further offence of the same type while on bail. Of the 83 persons charged with burglary who offended on bail, eight per cent committed an offence of car theft while on bail, 23 per cent committed an offence of theft (not of a car) and so on. These results agree with the picture that emerges from studies of criminal careers (Tarling, 1993).

Table 5.6 Court bail: original offences charged and offences committed while on bail

Original charge	Sample size	Offence committed on bail				
		Burglary	Car theft	Theft or handling	Violence or sex	Serious motoring
Burglary	83	*46%*	8%	23%	4%	4%
Car theft	50	20%	*28%*	12%	2%	18%
Theft or handling	107	8%	4%	*54%*	4%	8%
Violence or sex	43	14%	5%	21%	*21%*	9%
Serious motoring	20	10%	-	20%	5%	*35%*
Other offences	102	15%	12%	25%	10%	*4%*

---

7   The order of seriousness applied to the offences listed was: violence or sex offences, burglary, car theft, more serious motoring (i.e., reckless driving, driving while disqualified, or driving under the influence of alcohol or drugs) and theft or handling.

How frequently are individual defendants convicted of offences committed on bail?

The NIS records were used to count the number of times that defendants in the case tracking exercise were convicted of offences committed while they were on court bail. Of the 408 defendants who were convicted at least once of such an offence, nearly three-quarters were convicted once only, a sixth were convicted twice, five per cent were convicted three times and five per cent were convicted four or more times (see Table 5.7).

Table 5.7 Court bail: number of times convicted of offences committed while on bail

	Number of times convicted				
---	1	2	3	4 or more	Total
Number of defendants	301	66	22	19	408
Percentage	74%	16%	5%	5%	100%

6 Conclusions

The aim of this project was to identify ways of improving the information that was available to remand decision-makers. It was argued that, with better information, the police, CPS prosecutors, and magistrates should be better able to identify defendants who were likely to offend on bail, and to make recommendations/decisions on this basis. The effect would then be a reduction in the incidence of offending on bail.

The local steering groups identified several issues on which the information available to remand decision-makers was deficient (Appendix A gives more details) and sought changes to remedy these deficiencies. The possible changes fell into three categories:

• Changes which were needed at a national level, i.e. to improve access to criminal records and the detail that was available about past convictions. (No major improvements were possible until the new computerised system – Phoenix – became operational in 1995 and existing records had been converted. In the meantime, some local improvements in access were made in three of the court areas.)

• Changes which required additional resources – to set up additional bail information schemes, bail support schemes, a fostering scheme for juveniles on remand, and diversion schemes for mentally disordered offenders. (One prison based bail information scheme, one bail support scheme and one scheme for mentally disordered offenders were started within the project time scale but barely had time to show effects. Four other such schemes were planned but could not be started within the time scale.)

• More modest changes which could be implemented locally with current resources. The changes implemented included additional training courses for magistrates and custody officers in risk assessment; changes in the wording of conditions applied to bail; changes in court listing to allow more discussion between agencies before the first remand hearing, and changes in the records kept in court to include the arguments made in bail applications.

The rates of offending on bail were measured in each area before and after the changes were made. A reduction in offending on bail was found in two areas, in Horseferry Road (in central London) and in Leicester: there were no significant changes in the other three.

In Horseferry Road, the offending on court bail conviction rate decreased overall from 18 per cent in 1993 to 11 per cent in 1994. Although several actions were taken in the Horseferry Road area (see Chapter 2) it seems likely that the reduction in offending on bail resulted from the fact that more defendants were remanded in custody by the court: the custody rate increased from 18 per cent in 1993 to 24 per cent in 1994, six percentage points. Higher increases in the custody rates were found for defendants who fell into the categories shown to be at higher risk of offending on bail (those charged with certain categories of offence, and those who had served a custodial sentence in the past and who had breached bail in the past). It seems likely that the focus of the project on the topic of offending on bail caused magistrates to grant bail in fewer cases, and that this reduced the rates of offending on bail.

In Leicester the picture was rather different. While the offending on court bail conviction rate decreased from 20% in 1993 to 12% in 1994, this cannot be explained by higher custody rates or by changes in defendants' characteristics: there was a shift away from custody towards more unconditional bail (the custody rate decreased from 15% in 1993 to 10% in 1994). It seems, then, that the effects in Leicester may have been caused by the changes made. It is not possible to deduce precisely what the effect of individual changes were, since several were made at the same time. Also, similar changes were made in other areas which did not show the same effect. However, Leicester court did make a considerable investment in the training of bench chairmen, using the Magistrates' Association 'Bail Risk Exercise', and was the only court to take part in the special exercise directed by Professor Hassett to explore the approach taken by remand decision-makers to the assessment of risk.

The offending on court bail conviction rates in Bournemouth, Newport and Salford showed no change, a small decrease, and a small increase respectively. A change was observed in Newport regarding current offence details. In the case tracking exercise in 1993, magistrates reported that insufficient detail was provided regarding the current offence. No such comments were received in 1994, which suggests that some improvement had been made in this respect.

Over all five areas that took part in the project, the offending on court bail conviction rate was 20 per cent in 1993 and decreased to 15 per cent in 1994. The offending on court bail charge rate decreased from 23 per cent in

1993 to 20 per cent in 1994. These conviction rates are higher than those found in earlier police and Home Office research (Morgan, 1992), which gave percentages for 1986/89 ranging from 10 per cent to 17 per cent (the 17% figure included offences taken into consideration and cautions). However, some of this increase is likely to be explained by the fact that, in the Bail Process Project, only defendants who were found guilty of the original offence could be followed up for offending on bail.[1]

Analysis of the case tracking data for 1993 and 1994 showed which factors were associated with higher and lower rates of offending on court bail (Tables 5.2 and 5.3), namely, homelessness, the current offence, the previous criminal record, previous behaviour on bail, age, unemployment and the waiting time for trial. An equivalent group of factors were identified as being associated with higher or lower rates of remand in custody by the courts (Table 4.1) This suggests that, in the main, magistrates *were* targeting those defendants who were more likely to offend on bail. However, there were some important differences:

- the defendant's age does not seem to have affected the custody rate consistently, whereas it did affect the offending on bail rate (younger defendants were more likely to offend on bail)

- the offence categories that most attracted custodial remands included the more serious violence offences (GBH) and indictable/either way sex offences, whereas neither of these groups showed high rates of offending on bail.

- the waiting time for trial was not a factor in the bail/custody decision (for obvious reasons) whereas the offending on bail rates increased steadily as the waiting times increased.

Comparison of Tables 4.1 and 5.3 shows that magistrates *did* remand more defendants in custody from those groups with higher rates of offending on bail. In consequence, fewer were granted bail in these groups and hence the highest offending on bail rates relate to small samples of defendants (e.g. 63% of 32 homeless defendants charged with burglary, robbery or car theft offended on bail, as did 44% of 73 defendants charged with the same offences who had served a custodial sentence and had breached bail in the past). However, if all of these defendants had been remanded in custody, a third to one-half would have been in custody unnecessarily.

---

1   Although it is not certain what effect this change has on the rates of offending on bail, it is likely that it produces higher rates. No criminal record could be found for around a tenth of defendants, so they were not included as the period they were on bail was not known (see Appendix C). However, they presumably did not offend on bail or there would have been a criminal record. Hence the bail Process Project will produce higher figures for offending on bail than were found in earlier projects.

The larger groups of defendants in the samples followed up were those charged with offences other than burglary, robbery or car theft, who had not served a custodial sentence and who had not breached bail in the past. Of these, 16 per cent of (nearly 300) under-21s and six per cent of (the 760) adults in this category offended on bail. Put another way, one in six under-21s and one in 16 adults in the group offended on bail.

To avoid unnecessary remands in custody, and to reduce offending on bail, magistrates must target the two out of three (in the highest risk group) and the one in 16 in the lowest risk group. Such targeting might be based on information over and above the broader categories described: perhaps more detail of the current offence and how it relates to the criminal record to indicate a pattern of offending, an indication of the attitude of the defendant, and any circumstances or influences which may have a positive affect on future behaviour. However, even if such information were available, there is no guarantee that accurate predictions of offending would be possible. Another relevant factor is the waiting time before trial: the research has shown that longer waiting times are related to higher offending on bail. This suggests that, if changes in procedure or practice can be devised to reduce the waiting times for defendants on bail, there should be a corresponding reduction in offending on bail. Broad estimates suggest that a reduction in waiting times of around one month should correspond to a decrease of three per cent in offending on bail.

Appendix A Bail process:
a composite narrative map

This appendix summarises the main findings from the observations and consultations undertaken in 1993 by the Project Consultant, John Burrows, in the five project areas – Horseferry Road (London), Leicester, Salford, Poole/Bournemouth and Newport. It highlights:

• the differences in practice between the five areas

• practitioners' perceptions of the framework in which they operate

• perceived shortcomings

• possible best practice.

A. FROM ARREST TO CHARGE

The first stage in the bail process is the custody officer's decision on police bail under Section 38 or 47 of the Police and Criminal Evidence Act 1984 (PACE). Subsequent bail decisions in the courts are often influenced by the original police decision. *The selection and training of custody officers therefore has a strong bearing on all bail decisions.*

The staffing of custody suites varies from area to area, as does the type and extent of checks made into a defendant's identity, address and employment.

Knowledge of a defendant's antecedents is important and the sources for this may vary in range and reliability. This information may show details of offending behaviour including offending on bail but it is not unusual for the custody officer to make his decision without antecedents. *Antecedents inform the bail decision at all stages, not just in the police station, but, until the National Criminal Records System (NCRS) comes into operation,[1] there is little that can be done nationally to standardise the accessibility and currency of the information available to the police and the Crown Prosecution Service (CPS).*

---

1   This came into operation in May 1995

Custody officers feel they are very much in the firing line when making their bail decisions and that of all those making recommendations or decisions on bail – from the CPS to a judge in chambers – they are the only ones who can be held personally liable for their actions. The relevant PACE provision for refusing bail – prevention of physical injury or loss or damage to property – is not as all embracing as the Bail Act 1976 which says bail may be refused to prevent offending on bail. *The majority of custody officers feel constrained by the provisions in PACE and doubt the improved guidance in the recent Home Office circular would give any additional protection against disciplinary proceedings.*

The police cannot set conditions when granting bail and some regard this as a backward step.[2] *In cases where bail cannot reasonably be refused under Section 38 of PACE but the custody officer is concerned about a defendant's behaviour, there is often informal "bargaining" with his/her solicitor to ensure that if he/she is granted police bail, he/she stays at an agreed location or complies with some other informal condition.*

B. CHARGE TO FIRST APPEARANCE

On first appearance in court a defendant will either be on police bail or have been remanded overnight in police custody.[2] *The CPS believe that it is extremely difficult to recommend a remand in custody or even conditional bail for any defendant who has been on police bail and attended court at the proper time.*

The preparation of police files and the transfer of these files to the CPS are governed by the Manual of Guidance formulated by the Working Group on Pre-Trial Issues (WGPTI). *Some areas take a more formal line than others on the time limits involved here. The difficulty, particularly for overnight cases, is that the CPS will sometimes know less about a case than the defence (who may well have been at the police station for the interview etc.) and that the arresting officer is not always available to give more strength to CPS arguments against bail.*

There are bail information schemes at Horseferry Road, Leicester and Bournemouth but, currently, not at Salford and Newport. Their function is to provide positive and verifiable information to the CPS and the defence. They may not, however, always be aware of police and CPS decisions/recommendations about bail until shortly before the court sits. *Clarification of their responsibilities regarding negative information would improve their standing with the police, in particular.*

---

2 Criteria for refusing bail were changed by the Criminal Justice and Public Order Act 1994, which also allowed the police to grant conditional bail.

The provision of bail hostels and bail support schemes varies between areas as does the extent to which they are used by the courts. Bail hostels should be seen as providing a fixed address and some sort of controlled regime for defendants who might otherwise have been remanded in custody. Newport has a particularly well regarded bail support scheme run by Barnardos for young offenders up to 17 years old. Other areas have similar schemes in the pipeline. *The local steering groups might be able to initiate action to encourage the establishment and use of such schemes, given appropriate funding.*

C. COURT PROCEEDINGS: FIRST APPEARANCES

The composition of the benches, whether lay or stipendiary, depends on local arrangements. Most lay magistrates are familiar with the Judicial Studies Board (JSB) bail decision making card and rely quite heavily on the clerk to guide them through the issues. The CPS often believe that the bench does not challenge a defence application for an adjournment often enough. Magistrates believe that they are able to remand in custody less often now the likelihood of imprisonment if convicted has been reduced by the Criminal Justice Act 1991. *The availability and quality of information at this stage, especially antecedents, is vital to assist the court in these areas.*

Many bail applications are uncontested and the magistrates seem to place considerable faith in the CPS recommendations. They are unlikely to probe further if the CPS do not object to bail. In general, antecedents are only provided for the bench if the CPS are recommending a remand in custody or conditions. *Some benches are more inclined to be more inquisitorial than others and stipendiaries are more likely to remand a defendant in custody overnight if they consider the information before them to be inadequate.*

There are differing views of the appropriateness and effectiveness of bail conditions. Reporting requirements are particularly unpopular with the police because they impose an extra burden on them. Conditions are often the product of pre-hearing negotiations between the CPS and the defence to arrive at a package that will prove acceptable to the court. *Whatever conditions are used they should be enforceable.*

D. "POLICING" COURT BAIL

The bail notices used in the project areas vary considerably but all serve the dual function of court record and information to the defendant of the requirements of his/her bail. *It is important that a defendant clearly understands what a grant of bail entails and some simplification of the form or separate notices might be appropriate.*

The procedures followed for breaches of bail conditions and failures to appear differ from area to area. Some breaches of conditions are dealt with when a defendant reappears but not complying with reporting conditions is pursued less consistently. Failure to appear on police bail is pursued by the police but in some quarters it is not considered worth the effort. Failure to appear on court bail is a matter for the CPS to put to the court.

E. SECOND AND SUBSEQUENT APPEARANCES

Co-ordination between court and prison based bail information schemes varies from area to area. It is generally accepted that prison staff have valuable expertise in assessing risk, not only for bail for remand prisoners but also for home leave etc. for convicted prisoners. The Bournemouth/Poole project, in particular, is to study the feasibility of drawing more extensively on information HMP Dorchester can give on those remand prisoners who may respond positively to bail. *The projects may be able to examine more widely the success of prison assessments in predicting future behaviour on bail.*

There is a reluctance by benches to overturn a previous court's decision on bail unless there is a clear change in circumstances. Presently, subsequent courts will have the bail record forms but no more detail on the arguments (if any) which led to the decision. Neither will the prosecutor always be the same at subsequent hearings. *Later this year (1993), however, new rules will require the clerk to take a note of contested bail applications which will then be kept with the case papers. Some concern has been expressed that this might turn subsequent bail applications into appeals rather than fresh hearings.*

There is no empirical evidence readily available of the number of successful defence applications to a judge in chambers. Neither do any of the courts have a system for reporting the results of these applications to the magistracy. If this were provided, there would have to be a precise record of why the magistrates reached their original decision and the reasons behind the judgement of the higher court.

F. ADDITIONAL ISSUES AFFECTING BAIL DECISIONS FOR JUVENILES

When a person aged 16 or under is arrested the custody officer must ensure that an appropriate adult – either a parent or social worker – is present at the police station for the interview. Checks on antecedents and so on are conducted as for adults and the majority will be released on police bail. All five areas have similar juvenile/youth justice teams which review most cases against young defendants and decide whether to prosecute or caution. *These teams are a good example of agencies co-operating and exchanging all the information they have about a defendant, something which does not always seem to happen with adult defendants.*

All courts report a change in remands for young people since the introduction of the youth court. There is some confusion over 17-year-olds who, whilst they are dealt with in the youth court, are still treated as adults for bail. Magistrates also express concern that when the court remands a defendant aged 16 or under to local authority care this invariably means he/she goes back to the family home. *The provisions in the Criminal Justice Act 1991 regarding juvenile remands and the use of local authority secure accommodation strengthen magistrates powers but, in some areas, is a source of friction between the courts and the social services.*

Home Office
1993

Appendix B Sample cases used in the Leicester bail rule project

EXAMPLE 1: AMY ADAMS: AGE 18: ETHNIC ORIGIN – white European

OFFENCE: Three charges of theft from shops amounting to £58.

Is a single parent living in a council flat with her one-year-old child. Lives on state benefits. Has several similar convictions and failed to answer bail on one occasion.

EXAMPLE 2: BEN BROWN: AGE 26: ETHNIC ORIGIN – white European

OFFENCE: Theft of £5,000 worth of goods from employer.

Subsequently lost his job and the accommodation that went with it. Is now unemployed and has no fixed abode. Is divorced and has a problem with alcohol. Has no previous convictions.

EXAMPLE 3: CHARLES CARTER: AGE 20: ETHNIC ORIGIN – white European

OFFENCE: Assaulted girlfriend causing injuries of a cut lip, a black eye and bruises. They have been living together for two years in rented accommodation.

Has a job. Has several previous convictions mainly for public order offences. Six months ago, he was convicted of an identical assault. Has parents living in the area who would accommodate him if necessary.

EXAMPLE 9: CLIFFORD CARTER: AGE 24: ETHNIC ORIGIN – white European

OFFENCE: Assaulted girlfriend causing injuries of a cut lip, a black eye and bruises. They have been living together for two years in rented accommodation.

Is unemployed. Has no previous convictions. Has parents living in the area who would accommodate him if necessary.

EXAMPLE 4: DAVID DAVIS: AGE 18: ETHNIC ORIGIN – white European

OFFENCE: Grievous bodily harm. The defendant and victim were involved in a fight in a pub in which the defendant used a broken glass as a weapon. The victim spent a week in hospital recovering from his injuries. It is not clear who started the fight.

Is unemployed and lives with his parents. Has no previous convictions.

EXAMPLE 10: DONALD DAVIS: AGE 26: ETHNIC ORIGIN – white European

OFFENCE: Grievous bodily harm. The defendant and victim (an Asian youth of 22) were involved in a fight in a pub in which the defendant used a broken glass as a weapon. The victim spent a week in hospital recovering from his injuries.

The defendant will contest the charge. He claims that the victim started the fight and that he acted in self defence. Owns his own house. Has a job. Has three previous convictions for public order offences. Failed to appear on one occasion. Is a heavy drinker. The offence seems to have been committed when the defendant was under the influence of alcohol. Friends of the victim (also Asian) who witnessed the incident are nervous about giving evidence because they say they are afraid of the defendant and his drinking companions.

EXAMPLE 5: EVAN EDWARDS: AGE 19: ETHNIC ORIGIN – white European

OFFENCE: Burglary in a dwelling house and theft of electronic equipment, jewellery and personal papers, valued together at £2,000. The offence was committed during the night when the owners were away. The property was not recovered.

A witness saw two men leaving the house but the second man has not been identified. Is unemployed and has no fixed address. Has three previous convictions, two of which were for burglary. Failed to surrender to bail on one occasion.

EXAMPLE 11: ERROL EDWARDS: AGE 25: ETHNIC ORIGIN – Afro-Caribbean

OFFENCE: Burglary in a dwelling house and theft of electronic equipment, jewellery and personal papers, valued together at £2,000. The offence was committed during the night when the owners were away. The property was not recovered.

Was seen in the vicinity of the house earlier in the evening. Says that he was on the way to a friend's house. Denies the offence strongly and says he has been wrongly accused because he is known to the police. He intends to contest the case in the Crown Court. Is unemployed and lives with his mother in a rented flat. Has several previous convictions for possession of drugs and burglary. Has always surrendered to bail in the past.

Appendix C Methodology and problems

The five police forces who took part in the Bail Process Project recorded details for each defendant who was charged with an imprisonable offence in the six months April to June, 1993 and January to March, 1994. The information recorded included the charges brought; the police assessment of the risks of failing to appear, offending while on bail and interfering with witnesses; the police bail/custody decision; the reasons for the decision; and the date of arrest. A copy of the form completed for the NIS on arrest (NIB74A) was also provided: this gave some information about the defendant, i.e., age, nationality, race, circumstances of offence, home address, employment status and dates of offence and first court appearance.

The appropriate CPS branches categorised cases into three types:

- those in which there was no court remand before conviction/acquittal (i.e., the defendants were dealt with at the first court appearance): no details were recorded in these cases

- those in which police, CPS and court all agreed on unconditional bail ('agreed bail cases'): copies of selected police MG forms were provided, giving details of the defendant's age, nationality, address and employment status, criminal record, whether on bail in connection with other charges, and any known breaches of bail

- those in which there was a court remand and unconditional bail was *not* agreed by all parties: in addition to the copies of the selected MG forms described above, the CPS completed a cover sheet giving details of the remand recommendations made at the first two court hearings and the reasons for these, together with their assessments of the police bail/custody decision, the likelihood of a custodial sentence, the risk of the defendant failing to appear, offending on bail, and interfering with witnesses. The existence and usefulness of any bail information collected was also noted.

The court clerk completed a folder for cases in the third category above only. At the first two remand hearings, details were recorded of the decisions of the court and also any information presented to the magistrates by prosecution or defence. In addition, the magistrates completed a form at each hearing giving their reasons for the decision made, their assessments of the likelihood of a custodial sentence, and the risk of the defendant failing to appear, offending on bail, and interfering with witnesses.

After the second remand hearing or the date the defendant was dealt with, whichever was the earlier, the CPS and court recording forms were returned to the Home Office. By this means, it was known who was granted bail at either the first or the second hearing. The reasons for not continuing the recording until all cases were finally dealt with were first, to limit the extra work imposed on the CPS and courts and, second, to ensure that the details recorded were returned within a reasonable period after the end of the three months. (Otherwise, details of cases with long waiting times would not have been received for months or years, and these were likely to be the cases in which offending while on bail was more likely.) Those cases in which bail was granted at the first or second hearing were included in the offending on bail study.

In 1995 and early 1996, researchers worked at the National Identification Service at Scotland Yard to search for any offences which defendants in the samples had committed while they were on bail. It was necessary first to find the dates on which cases were finally dealt with, so that the periods defendants were on bail could be identified. The researchers then recorded details of any charges which were brought within these periods and whether they resulted in a conviction.

Problems with measuring offending on bail

Around 7,000 cases were followed up at NIS. No criminal records were found for 11 per cent of these. For a further 21 per cent, a criminal record was found but the offence recorded in 1993 or 1994 was not found on it. This meant that, for about one-third of cases, no date of disposal could be found to give the end of the period on court bail and, hence, no information could be found as to whether or not the defendant offended on court bail.

There are three possible reasons for no records of the offences charged being found at NIS. First, the defendant may not have been convicted of the offence: by definition, a criminal record is only held if the defendant is found guilty. Second, the offence charged might have been a non-standard list offence, i.e., an offence that is not on the list of offences that must be reported by the police to NIS – examples of such offences are driving while disqualified or driving under the influence of drink or drugs (although many of the first of these offences were found to be recorded). A third reason is that the requisite forms might not have been received by NIS at the time the searches were made. To minimise the last problem the NIS searches were not started until January 1995 for the 1993 sample, and August 1995 for the 1994 sample (thus allowing periods of 18 months and 16 months respectively for the case to be completed and the information to be passed on).[1]

A result of the methodology used was that offending on court bail could only be studied for defendants who were convicted of the original or target offence. This means that the results are not directly comparable with the results of earlier studies of offending while on court bail, which studied all defendants granted bail during a period (Home Office, 1981), Ennis and Nichols, 1991; Northumbria Police, 1991; Henderson and Nichols, 1992; and Morgan, 1992). Although the effects are uncertain, it seems likely that the offending on court bail rates for defendants found guilty (i.e. in the Bail Process Project) will be higher than the rates for all defendants granted bail. (The argument here is based on the 11% of defendants for whom no criminal records could be found: these were excluded because the date of the end of the bail period was not known. However, if they had been found guilty of a reportable offence committed while they were on bail, they would have had a criminal record. Hence, the omission of these cases will increase the apparent rates of offending while on bail.)

The problem described above does *not* apply to measures of offending while on police bail after charge. The start and finish dates for this type of bail were recorded by the police and the CPS respectively. Hence the records at NIS were searched for any offences committed during these periods regardless of whether the defendant was found guilty of the original offence.

Multiple appearances – offending on bail

Some defendants were charged and granted bail on more than one occasion during the three-month periods. In many cases, the second sets of charges were offences committed while on bail, and bail granted for these offences totally or largely overlapped the original period of bail.[2] The period chosen for police bail was the period which started on the first police date of charge within each three-month period. The period chosen for court bail was the

---

[1]   Because fewer of the 1994 records were found at NIS, an additional search was made for disposal dates from the Home Office Offenders Index for 1994/95. About 100 matches were found.

[2]   This was probably because the recording periods were relatively short (three months) compared to the interval between remand hearings (around one month).

period which started on the first court remand date in the three-month period, and for which there was a conviction. To test the effects of this methodology on the offending on bail rates, alternative rates were calculated when *all the known periods of police or court bail* (as appropriate) were included, and any overlapping ignored. In this way some offences were counted twice in different periods of bail. However, the rates differed from the rates given in this report by less than one percentage point. (The explanation is that a relatively small proportion of defendants in the samples had multiple sets of proceedings.)

Multiple appearances – court decision-making

For both police and court decisions, it was possible to include more than one remand decision made for individual defendants. However, because there was likely to be some correlation between such decisions, the results given in this paper are based on the first police decision made and the first court remand decision made. Again the effects of this methodology were tested by recalculating decision rates when all sets of proceedings were included. The differences were very small.

Appendix D Bail information

Three of the five areas that took part in the Bail Process Project had court based bail information schemes. In two of these, Bournemouth and Leicester, the bail information was collected from defendants held in police custody before the first court appearance. In the third, Horseferry Road, the information was collected after the first and before the second court appearance. In addition, some information was collected in Newport and Salford as part of juvenile liaison schemes, bail support schemes or by court probation officers.

CPS record

As part of the case tracking exercise, the CPS recorded information about the schemes that operated at the first court appearance.

For cases in which there was a court remand, and which were not 'agreed bail' cases, prosecutors were asked *'Was additional information on the defendant supplied from a bail information scheme or similar?'* Bail information only arises for defendants held in police custody. Of 301 such cases in Bournemouth, additional information was provided in 21 per cent (17% from bail information schemes, 2% from juvenile liaison schemes and 2% from other schemes). In Leicester, additional information was provided in 20 per cent of 306 cases involving police custody (19% from bail information schemes).

Prosecutors were then asked *'How would you rate the importance of the information provided to your recommendation to the court?'*. Table D.1 summarises the responses received.

Table D.1 CPS assessment of the usefulness of bail information

Rating	Bournemouth	Leicester
Very important	64%	57%
Quite important	15%	20%
Not very important	13%	18%
Of no value	8%	5%
Number of cases	61	60

In both areas, the additional information provided was regarded as very important or quite important in four out of five cases.

Bail information record

As part of the case tracking exercise, bail information officers were asked to complete a short form when they had made enquiries about a defendant. The 1993 sample consisted of 531 cases, the 1994 sample 550 cases. The majority of these were from Bournemouth and Leicester, with around 100 forms being received from Horseferry Road over the two years. Furthermore, some recording forms were also completed by the probation service in the two areas that did not have bail information schemes (around 100 from Newport and 60 from Salford in the two years).

The first question asked what enquiries had been carried out with respect to each individual defendant. Table D.2 summarises the responses received for both 1993 and 1994 taken together.

Table D.2 Enquiries that were carried out

Source of information	Percentage of cases
Interview with defence lawyer	83%
Interview with defendant	82%
Interview with CPS lawyer	69%
Telephone calls to possible places of accommodation	40%
Telephone enquiries to defendant's home	8%
Home visit	2%
Other	19%
Number of cases	1,081

Note: the percentages add to more than 100 because, in most cases, more than one enquiry was made.

Next, bail information officers were asked which agencies were given the results of the enquiries that they had made. The responses are shown in Table D.3 below.

Table D.3 Which agencies received the results of the enquiries

Agency	Percentage of cases
Defence	79%
CPS	67%
Court (direct)	30%
No agency	13%
No detail given	5%
Number of cases	1,081

Note: the percentages add to more than 100 because the information was often given to more than one agency.

When no agency was given the information, respondents were asked for more details. This usually occurred when bail had not been opposed (the most common reason), when there had been no bail application made, when the defendant's address had been confirmed by another agency (the police or defence solicitor), when the officer was 'not asked' for the information or 'no input was required' (which presumably means that there was no opportunity to provide information). In other cases, no enquiries had been made or no positive, verified information had been found.

Respondents were then asked what type of information was obtained. Table D.4 shows the responses obtained.

Table D.4 Type of information found in favour of bail in 1993 and 1994

Type	Percentage of cases
Details of alternative accommodation	46%
Details of home circumstances/family	32%
Other	19%
No type given	16%
Number of cases	1,081

Note: the percentages add to more than 100 because more than one category was appropriate in some cases.

Negative information, or information which would not support the defendant in seeking bail, was discussed in some of the local steering groups. The police were concerned that, if the bail information officer obtained such information, it should be made available to the CPS or the court. In consequence, respondents were asked *'Did any information that would not favour bail come to light during your enquiries?'* The answer was 'Yes' in 126 (12%) of the 1,081 cases recorded in 1993 and 1994. For these cases, respondents were asked who the negative information was passed to. The responses are given in Table D.5.

Table D.5 Information found that would not favour bail: to whom it was passed

Agency	Percentage of cases
Defence lawyer	77%
CPS	62%
Police	12%
No-one	14%
Number of cases	103

Note: the percentages add to more than 100 because the information was usually passed to more than one agency.

Appendix E Bail provisions of the Criminal Justice and Public Order Act 1994: some small scale evaluations

The effects of the CJPO Act, 1994

The Criminal Justice and Public Order Act (CJPO), 1994, introduced six new bail measures in light of the concern about the extent of offending on bail. The new measures aimed to tighten up the granting of bail and gave the police and the courts new powers to deal with abuse of bail. All six measures came into force on 10 April 1995.

The 1994 Act provides that anyone charged with murder, attempted murder, rape, attempted rape or manslaughter who has a previous conviction for any of these offences, or for culpable homicide, shall not be granted bail by the police or the courts and must be remanded in custody (s25). It also includes a measure providing no right to bail for a person charged with an indictable only or triable either way offence if it appears that the defendant was already on bail when the alleged offence was committed (s26). There are also specific new powers for the police to grant conditional bail after charge (s27), to deny bail in order to prevent further offending (s28) and to arrest without warrant a defendant who fails to answer police bail to return to the police station (s29). The final measure introduced powers for the court, on application by the prosecution, to reconsider a bail decision before a defendant's next scheduled appearance where new information relevant to the bail decision comes to light, and to impose or vary bail conditions or revoke bail in such circumstances (s30).

Three studies were carried out in 1995/6 to assess the effects of some of the new powers given to the police and the courts. These took the form of:

(i) a survey of the views of custody officers in the five Bail Process Project areas, to assess how far the new provisions (in s27–29) had satisfied the problems expressed by these officers in an earlier survey in 1993;[1]

(ii) a study of the effects of s26 of the Act on remand decisions in Leicester court. Decisions made for defendants who were on bail when charged with a further offence, during a four-month period, were compared with corresponding decisions monitored as part of the Bail Process Project case tracking exercise in 1994;[2]

(iii) a study similar to (ii) in Bournemouth and Poole courts.[3]

A summary of the findings follows. More detailed reports are available from Information and Publications Group, Room 201, Home Office, 50 Queen Anne's Gate, London SW1H 9AT.

Custody Officers Study

The new provisions were greatly desired in the earlier 1993 study of custody officers, so it is not surprising that they have been widely welcomed now that they are in place.

The power to arrest police bail defaulters was reported as used in all the areas surveyed. It was not used in the cases of all defendants who fail to return to the police station, and there was no clear pattern in the selection of the cases to which it is applied. The main problem with the power itself appeared to be some confusion over whether there was a related power of entry to effect the arrest. The main benefits were perceived to be a clarification of legislation and the fact that the new power was encouraging defendants to answer police bail. A few problems were mentioned regarding the operation of juvenile panels, which were seen as a source of delay and sometimes inconsistency, and several officers also thought bail to return to the station was being over-used.

---

1   This was carried out by Henderson as part of the Bail Process Project – see Burrows, Henderson and Morgan, 1994.

2   This research was carried out by Anthea Hucklesby and Emma Marshall, University of Leicester, under contract to the Home Office.

3   This research was carried out by Jenny Warren under contract to the Home Office.

The new criterion for deciding whether or not to withhold bail was also reported to be in wide use, and was already among the most popular of the criteria available to custody officers. Many officers said that its main benefit was its application to cases involving persistent offenders who had not previously been covered, so that many of these offenders were now held in custody rather than bailed. It seems likely that much of the enthusiasm for the new provision arises from the removal of the sense of vulnerability previously felt by custody officers who considered that the original criteria did not offer sufficient support should their decision be challenged.

The power to apply conditions to bail after charge was widely welcomed and reported to be in regular use. It was seen to bring such benefits as savings in court and police time. A condition requiring defendants to keep away from a named person was particularly frequently used. However, some problems were also reported, particularly with the dissemination of information about the conditions to other police staff. It seemed, too, that there are applications being made to the police for variation in conditions applied by custody officers, and this is an aspect of police conditions that may require some attention and clarification. There are also indications that some defendants who would hitherto have been released on unconditional bail (perhaps reluctantly) were being given bail with conditions.

Training remained a problem in some areas. Most of the areas surveyed appeared to have held some training courses for custody officers in the run-up to the introduction of the new powers, although this does not seem to be the case in Dorset and Manchester. Few of the officers had received specific training in bail decision-making. Most of the respondents felt that they would benefit from further training. The 1993 study reported similar findings; training in bail decision-making still remains to be addressed.

Leicester Court Study

Table E.1 Court Remand Decisions Before and After the Implementation of the CJPO Act 1994: defendants on bail when charged with a further offence

	Before	*After*
Unconditional Bail	58%	37%
Conditional Bail	17%	34%
Remand in Custody	21%	23%
Under 18 Care/Remand in Custody	4%	6%
Total (n=)	217	423

Table E.1 shows that the main impact of the CJPO Act 1994 appears to be a shift from the grant of unconditional bail to conditional bail. This may be explained by the impact of s26 or by other factors, in particular the new police power to attach conditions to police bail enshrined in s27 of the Act.

The proportion of defendants remanded in custody only marginally increased. The increase was mainly accounted for by a slight increase in custody rates for less serious offences, suggesting that the courts already took account of seriousness of the offence charged prior to the Act. In other words, s26 has not changed court remand decisions in those cases which already were deemed to be serious.

The findings suggest that the nature and seriousness of the offence, previous bail and offending history and community ties all have an effect on magistrates' remand decisions. However, the importance of bail history seems to have increased in two ways since the introduction of the CJPO Act 1994. Firstly, the findings suggest that the increase in the use of conditional bail is more significant for defendants who have a bail history than those who do not. This indicates that the court is now more likely to restrict the liberty of defendants who have a bail history while still granting them bail. Secondly, defendants charged with more serious offences who have a bail history are more likely to be remanded in custody after the introduction of the Act.

The legal distinction between summary only offences on the one hand and either way and indictable only offences on the other which is enshrined in s26 does not seem to greatly influence the outcome of remand hearings. There was a similar shift to conditional bail for those charged with summary offences.

Several changes to the law on bail were enacted by the CJPO Act 1994 and no firm conclusions can be drawn about which provision is responsible for the changes found in this research. If any conclusion can be drawn, it must be that the legislative changes have affected both police and court decision making and that the decisions which they take seem to be based on similar criteria. In this sense, the bail provisions of the CJPO Act 1994 have been successful as one of their aims was to bring the criteria on which the police and courts base their remand decisions into line.

---

3   This research was carried out by Jenny Warren under contract to the Home Office.

Bournemouth and Poole Court Study

Table E.2 Court Remand Decisions Before and After the Implementation of the CJPO Act 1994: defendants on bail when charged with a further offence

	Before	*After*
Unconditional Bail	42%	39%
Conditional Bail	35%	34%
Remand in Custody	23%	27%
Total (n=)	103	126

The proportion of defendants granted unconditional bail since the implementation of s26 of the CJPO Act 1994 showed a small fall of three per cent whilst those remanded in custody rose slightly by four per cent. The proportion of defendants given conditional bail remained unchanged. The increase in custody rate may be due to the introduction of s26 of the CJPO Act 1994 or to other factors. Interpretation of the results is difficult because of the small sample size, but the results tend to suggest that the implementation of s26 of the CJPO Act 1994 did not have a measurable effect on the decision-making process within the court.

Although many of the changes to the court remand process may have been due to other factors, there were indications that remand decisions since the implementation of the Act give greater weight to a defendants' offending history.

After implementation of s26 of the CJPO Act 1994:

- there were more court decisions to remand in custody

- the custody rate for 'more serious' offences decreased except where the defendant had four or more previous convictions or a previous custodial sentence (however the custody rate for 'more serious' offences remained high at 60%)

- the custody rate for 'less serious' offences increased, with other factors such as previous criminal history having more influence on the court decision

- defendants with more than four bail breaches were more likely to be remanded into custody

- defendants with more than four previous convictions were more likely to be remanded into custody.

References

Brookes S. (1991) *The effect of 're-offending' on bail on crime in Avon and Somerset.* Avon and Somerset Constabulary.

Burrows, J.N., Henderson, P.F. and Morgan, P.M. (1994) *Improving bail decisions: the Bail Process Project, phase 1.* Research and Planning Unit Paper 90. London: Home Office.

Ennis J. and Nichols T. (1991) *Offending on bail.* Metropolitan Police Directorate of Management Services Report No. 16/90. Metropolitan Police.

Godson, D. and Mitchell, C. (1991) *Bail information schemes in English magistrates' courts – a review of the data.* Inner London Probation Service, London. HMSO.

Greater Manchester Police (1988) *Offences committed on bail.* Research Paper: Greater Manchester Police.

Hassett, P. (1992) *Using expert system technology to improve bail decisions.* Research Working Papers. London: Institute of Advanced Legal Studies (University of London).

Henderson, P.F. and Nichols, T. (1992) *Offending while on bail.* Research Bulletin, No. 32. London: Home Office.

Henderson, P.F. (1998) *A survey of custody officers' views on new provisions of the Criminal Justice & Public Order Act 1994.* Home Office

Home Office (1981) *Estimates of offending by those on bail.* Statistical Bulletin No. 22/81. London: Home Office.

Hucklesby A. and Marshall, E. (1998) *Tackling offending on bail: the Impact of Section 26 of the Criminal Justice & Public Order Act 1994.* Home Office.

Lloyd, C. (1992) *Bail information schemes: practice and effect.* Research and Planning Unit Paper 69. London: Home Office.

Lloyd, C. and Mair, G.(1996) *Policy and progress in the development of bail schemes in England and Wales.* In: Paterson, F. (ed): Understanding bail in Britain. The Scottish Office Central Research Unit. London: HMSO.

Morgan, P.M. (1992) *Offending on bail: a survey of recent studies.* Research and Planning Unit Paper 65. London: Home Office.

Morgan, P.M. and Pearce, R. (1989) *Remand decisions in Brighton and Bournemouth.* Research and Planning Unit Paper 53. London: Home Office.

Northumbria Police (1991) *Bail and multiple offending.* Research project 1990-91: Northumbria Police.

Raine J.R. and Willson, M.J. (1994) *Conditional bail or bail with conditions? (The use and effectiveness of bail conditions).* Birmingham University, School of Public Policy.

Raine J.R. and Willson, M. J. (1996) *Police bail with conditions? (The cost/savings effects of the new power).* Birmingham University, School of Public Policy.

Tarling R. (1993) *Analysing offending: data, models and interpretations.* London: HMSO.

Warren J. (1998) *Monitoring the effects of Section 26 of the Criminal Justice & Public Order Act 1994 in Bournemouth Magistrates Court.* Home Office.

Publications

List of research publications

A list of research reports for the last three years is provided below. A **full** list of publications is available on request from the Research and Statistics Directorate Information and Publications Group.

Home Office Research Studies (HORS)

151. **Drug misuse declared: results of the 1994 British Crime Survey.** Malcom Ramsay and Andrew Percy. 1996.

152. **An Evaluation of the Introduction and Operation of the Youth Court.** David O'Mahony and Kevin Haines. 1996.

153. **Fitting supervision to offenders: assessment and allocation decisions in the Probation Service.** 1996.

154. **Ethnic minorities: victimisation and racial harassment.** Marian FitzGerald and Chris Hale. 1996.

155. **PACE: a review of the literature. The first ten years.** David Brown. 1997.

156. **Automatic Conditional Release: the first two years.** Mike Maguire, Brigitte Perroud and Peter Raynor. 1996.

157. **Testing obscenity: an international comparison of laws and controls relating to obscene material.** Sharon Grace. 1996.

158. **Enforcing community sentences: supervisors' perspectives on ensuring compliance and dealing with breach.** Tom Ellis, Carol Hedderman and Ed Mortimer. 1996.

160. **Implementing crime prevention schemes in a multi-agency setting: aspects of process in the Safer Cities programme.** Mike Sutton. 1996.

161. **Reducing criminality among young people: a sample of relevant programmes in the United Kingdom.** David Utting. 1997.

162. **Imprisoned women and mothers.** Dianne Caddle and Debbie Crisp. 1996.

163. **Curfew orders with electronic monitoring: an evaluation of the first twelve months of the trials in Greater Manchester, Norfolk and Berkshire, 1995 – 1996.** George Mair and Ed Mortimer. 1996.

164. **Safer cities and domestic burglaries.** Paul Ekblom, Ho Law, Mike Sutton, with assistance from Paul Crisp and Richard Wiggins. 1996.

165. **Enforcing financial penalties.** Claire Whittaker and Alan Mackie. 1997.

166. **Assessing offenders' needs: assessment scales for the probation service.** Rosumund Aubrey and Michael Hough. 1997.

167. **Offenders on probation.** George Mair and Chris May. 1997.

168. **Managing courts effectively: The reasons for adjournments in magistrates' courts.** Claire Whittaker, Alan Mackie, Ruth Lewis and Nicola Ponikiewski. 1997.

169. **Addressing the literacy needs of offenders under probation supervision.** Gwynn Davis et al. 1997.

170. **Understanding the sentencing of women.** edited by Carol Hedderman and Lorraine Gelsthorpe. 1997.

171. **Changing offenders' attitudes and behaviour: what works?** Julie Vennard, Darren Sugg and Carol Hedderman 1997.

172. **Drug misuse declared in 1996: latest results from the British Crime Survey.** Malcolm Ramsay and Josephine Spiller. 1997.

173. **Ethnic monitoring in police forces: A beginning.** Marian FitzGerald and Rae Sibbitt. 1997.

174. **In police custody: Police powers and suspects' rights under the revised PACE codes of practice.** Tom Bucke and David Brown. 1997.

176. **The perpetrators of racial harassment and racial violence.** Rae Sibbitt. 1997.

177. **Electronic monitoring in practice: the second year of the trials of curfew orders.** Ed Mortimer and Chris May. 1997.

179.   **Attitudes to punishment: findings from the British Crime Survey.**
        Michael Hough and Julian Roberts. 1998.

No. 159, 175 and 178 are not published yet.

Research Findings

30.   **To scare straight or educate? The British experience of day visits
        to prison for young people.** Charles Lloyd. 1996.

31.   **The ADT drug treatment programme at HMP Downview – a
        preliminary evaluation.** Elaine Player and Carol Martin. 1996.

32.   **Wolds remand prison – an evaluation.** Keith Bottomley, Adrian James,
        Emma Clare and Alison Liebling. 1996.

33.   **Drug misuse declared: results of the 1994 British Crime Survey.**
        Malcolm Ramsay and Andrew Percy. 1996.

34.   **Crack cocaine and drugs-crime careers.** Howard Parker and   Tim
        Bottomley. 1996.

35.   **Imprisonment for fine default.** David Moxon and Claire Whittaker.
        1996.

36.   **Fine impositions and enforcement following the Criminal Justice
        Act 1993.** Elizabeth Charman, Bryan Gibson, Terry Honess and Rod
        Morgan. 1996.

37.   **Victimisation in prisons.** Ian O'Donnell and Kimmett Edgar. 1996.

38   **Mothers in prison.** Dianne Caddle and Debbie Crisp. 1997.

39.   **Ethnic minorities, victimisation and racial harassment.** Marian
        Fitzgerald and Chris Hale. 1996.

40.   **Evaluating joint performance management between the police and
        the Crown Prosecution Service.** Andrew Hooke, Jim Knox and David
        Portas. 1996.

41.   **Public attitudes to drug-related crime.** Sharon Grace. 1996.

42.   **Domestic burglary schemes in the safer cities programme.** Paul
        Ekblom, Ho Law and Mike Sutton. 1996.

43. **Pakistani women's experience of domestic violence in Great Britain.** Salma Choudry. 1996.

44. **Witnesses with learning disabilities**. Andrew Sanders, Jane Creaton, Sophia Bird and Leanne Weber. 1997.

45. **Does treating sex offenders reduce reoffending?** Carol Hedderman and Darren Sugg. 1996.

46. **Re-education programmes for violent men - an evaluation.** Russell Dobash, Rebecca Emerson Dobash, Kate Cavanagh and Ruth Lewis. 1996.

47. **Sentencing without a pre-sentence report**. Nigel Charles, Claire Whittaker and Caroline Ball. 1997.

48. **Magistrates' views of the probation service.** Chris May. 1997.

49. **PACE ten years on: a review of the research**. David Brown. 1997.

50. **Persistent drug–misusing offenders.** Malcolm Ramsay. 1997.

51. **Curfew orders with electronic monitoring: The first twelve months.** Ed Mortimer and George Mair. 1997.

52. **Police cautioning in the 1990s.** Roger Evans and Rachel Ellis. 1997.

53. **A reconviction study of HMP Grendon Therapeutic Community.** Peter Marshall. 1997.

54. **Control in category C prisons.** Simon Marshall. 1997.

55. **The prevalence of convictions for sexual offending.** Peter Marshall. 1997.

56. **Drug misuse declared in 1996: key results from the British Crime Survey.** Malcolm Ramsay and Josephine Spiller. 1997.

57. **The 1996 International Crime Victimisation Survey.** Pat Mayhew and Phillip White. 1997.

58. **The sentencing of women: a section 95 publication.** Carol Hedderman and Lizanne Dowds. 1997.

Occasional Papers

Mental disorder in remand prisoners. Anthony Maden, Caecilia J. A. Taylor, Deborah Brooke and John Gunn. 1996.

An evaluation of prison work and training. Frances Simon and Claire Corbett. 1996.

The impact of the national lottery on the horse-race betting levy. Simon Field. 1996.

Evaluation of a Home Office initiative to help offenders into employment. Ken Roberts, Alana Barton, Julian Buchanan, and Barry Goldson. 1997.

The impact of the national lottery on the horse-race betting levy. Simon Field and James Dunmore. 1997.

Requests for Publications

Home Office Research Studies from 143 onwards, *Research and Planning Unit Papers, Research Findings and Research Bulletins* can be requested, **subject to availability**, from:

Research and Statistics Directorate
Information and Publications Group
Room 201, Home Office
50 Queen Anne's Gate
London SW1H 9AT
Telephone: 0171-273 2084
Fascimile: 0171-222 0211
Internet: http://www.open.gov.uk/home_off/rsd/rsdhome.htm
E-mail: rsd.ha apollo @ gtnet.gov.u.

Occasional Papers can be purchased from:
Home Office
Publications Unit
50 Queen Anne's Gate
London SW1H 9AT
Telephone: 0171 273 2302

Home Office Research Studies prior to 143 can be purchased from:

HMSO Publications Centre

(Mail, fax and telephone orders only)
PO Box 276, London SW8 5DT
Telephone orders: 0171-873 9090
General enquiries: 0171-873 0011
(queuing system in operation for both numbers)
Fax orders: 0171-873 8200

And also from **HMSO Bookshops**